The Way To Write Non-Fiction

By the same author in this series

The Way To Write Magazine Articles

The Way To Write
Non-Fiction

JOHN HINES

ELM TREE BOOKS · LONDON

ELM TREE BOOKS

Published by the Penguin Group
27 Wrights Lane, London w8 5TZ, England
Viking Penguin Inc., 40 West 23rd Street, New York, New York 10010, USA
Penguin Books Australia Ltd, Ringwood, Victoria, Australia
Penguin Books Canada Ltd, 2801 John Street, Markham, Ontario, Canada L3R 1B4
Penguin Books (NZ) Ltd, 182–190 Wairau Road, Auckland 10, New Zealand

Penguin Books Ltd, Registered Offices: Harmondsworth, Middlesex, England

First published in Great Britain by Elm Tree Books 1990

Made and printed in Great Britain by Richard Clay Ltd, Bungay, Suffolk
Filmset in Bembo

A CIP catalogue record for this book is available from the British Library

ISBN 0-241-12763-7

For my children, Nina, Catherine, Andrew and Stephen, and my wife, Molly — a family whose loving support has kept me writing, in spite of all the diverting demands of that outside world.

Contents

Chapter One

Making a start

Why non-fiction?

The field of non-fiction offers a wealth of opportunity for today's writers. The number of non-fiction books on the lists of most publishers far exceeds that of fiction and the publishers' demands for more non-fiction appear to be insatiable. The range of non-fiction subjects is almost infinite and many books can be written and re-written in a wide variety of ways.

In earning capacity, non-fiction books can often compete very favourably with all but the best-sellers in fiction. A very telling point in favour of non-fiction is the relative ease with which a new writer can obtain an advance contract for a saleable idea and a well-written synopsis, often with a substantial advance on royalties. This would be virtually impossible for a first novel.

Despite these advantages, new writers tend to turn their first efforts to fiction. They may regard it as more glamorous. They look at the best-sellers and imagine fiction as a possible source of wealth. They even see themselves as a household name.

It is true that many non-fiction books suffer somewhat from their lack of glamour. They can never win the Booker prize. In fact, there are relatively few major open awards for non-fiction.

Even the name 'non-fiction' describes what it is not, rather than what it is. So, it is hardly surprising that, in many people's eyes, non-fiction is eclipsed by the flood of fiction, much of which may be sensationalised and 'over-hyped'.

The facts are somewhat different. Fiction writing is hard

work, often for no return at all. It can mean years of graft with no guarantee of even modest returns. I know published novelists who earn very little from a book, sometimes less than a non-fiction writer might get for one first-class article.

If would-be authors are determined to see their names on the spine of a book, then they should consider non-fiction as the possible gateway to success. However, they should not see it as an easy option. Writing good non-fiction can be very demanding. Factual errors are more apparent and less readily forgiven than in fiction and serious omissions can bring harsh criticism. Indeed, some errors could be positively dangerous if they occurred in a manual of first-aid, deep-sea navigation or survival skills, for example.

Non-fiction is a field which includes works of the greatest importance, the writing of which can generate considerable personal satisfaction. Even if a writer's first inclination is to write fiction, many who turn to non-fiction maintain their success and never look back.

The non-fiction writer can usually achieve regular sales by writing magazine articles. This can be a valuable apprenticeship before taking on the more demanding task of writing books. Here again, non-fiction scores, for the fiction writer who tries to cut his teeth on short stories is up against a small and tight market. In addition, the very dissimilar techniques required for novels and short stories make the latter of little help as stepping-stones.

But magazine articles are ephemeral. They are on the shelves of bookshops for two or three weeks at the most, only to be replaced by the next issue. However well-written or beautifully illustrated the article may be, it only survives as the tear-sheets in the writer's files or in the dog-eared copies in doctors' and dentists' waiting rooms. A book is quite a different matter. It may not remain in print for more than two or three years, but it endures on private bookshelves and in public libraries for a very long time. Perhaps it is this longevity, with a hint of possible immortality, which makes the book so attractive to article and short story writers.

Although magazine-article writing represents a significant proportion of all non-fiction, it is not specifically dealt with in this book. Instead, I have concentrated on non-fiction books, which are the natural progression from magazine articles. The techniques of writing, selling and illustrating articles are covered in depth in my companion book, *The Way To Write Magazine Articles*.

A writer's accrued expertise in his specialist subjects is a valuable asset. It may include filed research material, contacts with experts or access to illustrations. It will almost certainly include the acquired skills in handling all this material and writing about it. It represents a heavy investment in time and money and it must be continually re-invested to the best possible advantage. To this end you must parcel it up in a wide variety of ways and sell it.

You may have already done this in the form of articles. Now look at it from a new angle as a potential author of books. In the following pages I shall show you how to do this effectively.

Finding the subject

What is it that triggers that germ of an idea for writing a first book? Where does the stimulus come from that sparks off the realisation that, for you, writing a book might not be a mere pipe-dream? Frequently, it is the subject itself which is the driving-force, rather than the need to write a book – any book.

My very first magazine article was on the making of fishing lures. It arose from a friend's suggestion that I should write a book on the subject. I rejected the idea because I felt I had insufficient material and, in any case, I was overawed at the thought of committing myself to a full-length book. Instead, I wrote an article.

Perhaps I was wrong. Not long after, Thurlow Craig, the well-known country writer, wrote his book *Baitmakers' Delight*. I could have written most of it from my own background knowledge, but it was Thurlow Craig's professionalism and my inexperience which dictated whose name should appear on the cover.

It was many years later that I wrote my first book. It arose from my passionate concern for wildlife conservation and the burning need to generate public concern for those much-maligned but delightful little animals – bats.

I had written dozens of articles, using hundreds of my own photographs. I knew my subject intimately. I had 95% of the material I needed for a book. I had the advantage of published articles in top quality magazines which should establish my credibility with a publisher. The first publisher I approached gave me a contract and paid an advance on royalties. I wrote the book with my wife, Molly, as co-author.

It happens this way for many writers. They, like us, find that it is the subject which is the motivator of their first book. I believe there is no better way to begin writing non-fiction books.

People say, 'I have nothing to write about.' Yet many successful books are written on simple everyday subjects, seen with sensitivity and often passion.

Those for whom the subject of a first book is self-evident are fortunate. They will already have a great deal of knowledge and material. This will cut down the necessary research and be easier than starting from scratch. Those who have no such obvious lead and yet feel the burning need to write a book, per se, will have to explore in other directions.

What do you know?

Every individual is unique. We have within ourselves a special amalgam of our nurture, our knowledge, our experience, our skills and all the overtones of what we call life. These colour our view of the world and nobody else sees it from precisely our viewpoint. Of course, there will be elements which stand out in our lives. It might be our career. Is it successful or unusual? Would our knowledge or experience be valuable or intriguing to others? Have we a special hobby or a craft? Would it fascinate others? Are there subjects on which we have done a great deal of reading? Have we already met with success in writing on one subject in particular?

Any of these factors could give you a strong lead when selecting a subject for that first book.

Personally, I would never start a book on a subject which didn't really interest me. It must capture my imagination. A good motto to have in mind is: 'Boring to write – boring to read.'

There are, of course, many professionals who can sit down and write to order on almost any subject. It is their job, their bread and butter. They admit that some of it is tedious, but they live in the hope that the next book will be fascinating.

I could never write in that way. Fortunately, I don't have to. I write for pleasure as well as money and I never lose sight of that fact.

However enthusiastic you may be about your subject, you must remember that a vital ingredient for success is saleability. Will others be fascinated by your book, not just a few others, but a great number, sufficient to make it a financial success? This is the prime question the publisher will be asking. It is something of a guessing game and even the experienced judgement of top publishers can prove to be flawed.

Checking the market

Unless your proposed subject is particularly unusual, there are steps you can take which go some way towards testing its saleability.

Although you may feel you have a fair idea of how popular your subject may be, it is unreliable to judge by the response of friends and family. You should check other books on the subject. How many are there in your library? Don't hesitate to ask your librarian's help.

Study those library books. Are they, in your opinion, attract-ive, well-written and clearly illustrated? Look at the date-stamps to see how often they are borrowed. If the last date-stamp was three years ago, ask yourself the reason. If they do appear to be good books, could it be the subject which is unappealing? In what way would your book be better? How much better? Would it be enough to make it more saleable?

Look at the date of publication. Has it been reprinted? Has it been revised? Check how frequently there have been reprints and revisions. If it is an old copy, you can ask the librarian to check up and see if it is still in print.

You should also have a look round a major bookshop. The large shops have computerised lists of all books in print and can give you the details in a few seconds. Don't be shy about asking the shop assistant how well a book is selling. An advantage of studying books in shops is that they indicate current trends, whereas the majority of books in libraries may well be out-of-date.

Also look at the bargain book shops which sell remaindered books. Check to see which books are having to be sold off cheaply because the publishers have over-estimated the demand.

Keep a note of every book you discover on your chosen subject and every aspect of it which might prove useful. If the factors are in your favour, your publisher will be interested to hear about them.

Some subjects may be too extensive to cover in this way and you will have to focus on a sub-classification which covers your specific field. For example, a teacher planning to write a school text-book on maths would have to consider his readers' age-group, the particular aspect of maths to be covered and even the proposed style. Is it to be a straight text-book or will it have a chatty style, full of everyday examples?

Those prolific subjects

Some subjects seem to dominate the bookshops and their variations appear to be inexhaustible. Gardening and cooking are two leading examples. Such subjects should never be ignored merely because there are plenty of books on them already available.

For example, if you look at a Victorian gardening book and a modern one, you will see few radical differences. Modern pesticides, herbicides and fertilisers, new hybrid strains, together with pretty pictures, are about the only things which differ very much. Gardens are dug the same, hoed the same, harvested the same. In general, seeds are still planted at the same time, at the same depth and the same way up. Yet modern gardening books explain in detail, with pictures, exactly how to dig the ground as if it is a revelation. They will continue to do so for many years to come.

Gardening writers lean heavily on a snappy title, a good cover or their reputations as TV gardening personalities. Others go for the oblique approach to the subject, using the same material, but linking it with a specialised aspect, some profound, some superficial.

Typical titles might be *Organic Gardening, No-dig Gardening, The Lazy Man's Gardening, The Wildlife Garden, The Natural Garden, Gardening without Tears, . . . without Sweat, . . . on £5 a year, . . . for only 15 minutes a week*. Or they could specialise in a particular flower, shrub or vegetable, *The Complete Manual on Tomato Growing*, for example.

Read these books and you will find they are, basically, the time-honoured knowledge of our grandfathers, with a top-dressing of modern tools and chemicals. Make no mistake, some of these books are very well written and they make money.

Books on cooking follow a similar pattern, from Mrs Beeton to specialised books for vegetarians, vegans, slimmers, diabetics, etc. There are books of Indian cooking, Chinese, Spanish and just about every nationality in the world. They focus on cooking methods, microwave, barbecue, no-fat, cooking for freezing and much more. There are books on cooking for one, for two, for the family, for children, for parties, for banquets and so on. One thing is certain, the publishers' hunger for original, near-original and big-name books on cooking will never wane.

Gardening and cooking are not the only subjects which seem to lend themselves to endless successful books. If you think about it, there are plenty of others, the self-help medical field being a particularly big one.

I have given these at some length to show how a theme can be written straight, fragmented, reslanted and, using the same basic material, earn its writer money for the rest of his life.

The beauty of being a specialist is that your material is all at hand. You only have to ensure that you are up-to-date with developments. As you write and rewrite on a subject, so your credibility grows. You are an expert and editors and publishers start approaching you.

Beware of topical subjects. Publishing a book is normally a slow business and subjects which will have only short-term sales potential are unlikely to appeal to publishers.

In examining some of the subjects and their sources, it will hardly be surprising if I have failed to cover your own speciality. After all, I said earlier that the range of subjects is almost infinite. This chapter is intended to be a stimulus to your own imagination, rather than a blueprint on precisely where to start.

The main points to remember are that there are many subjects from which to choose. Some will be easier for you to start with than others. Some have the potential which enables you to re-write time and again. Specialising can be a growth business which may pay handsomely.

Having provisionally decided on the subject of your first book, you must ask yourself a number of questions. Do you have sufficient material to sustain a book? If not, can you get it? Don't make a hurried decision here, for what may appear to be a very slight subject could still justify a book. I noticed recently that two books were published almost simultaneously on the subject of how to wrap gifts.

I re-emphasise that the vital question is whether such a book has a good sales potential. It will be the publisher who makes the final decision on this point, but you must make the best deduction you can from the facts available. After all, you will be investing quite a lot of time, even on the preliminaries, and you should be reasonably sure that your confidence isn't wildly misplaced.

Chapter Two

Finding a publisher

The preliminaries

You have chosen your subject and you have considered the material available. You must now think about the slant your book is to have. In other words, the way in which it will be different from others on the same subject. What will it include and, equally important, what will it leave out?

This is a good time to think about the chapter headings and consider what those chapters might contain. Only a rough idea is needed at this stage and it will be subject to amendment as you proceed.

Once you have a fairly clear idea of the shape of your book, you are ready for the next step, which is to consider approaching a publisher.

The prior contract

You may feel that, at this stage, it is a little premature to be looking for a publisher, but, in most cases, this is the correct time to do so. Providing that you have plenty of material, a sufficiently clear idea to enable you to draft a synopsis and a confidence in your ability to write the book, you are ready to find a publisher.

Far too many would-be authors write their books and then start the tedious task of peddling them round the publishing houses. This can be very slow and disappointing. Publishers may keep your MS for months before making a decision. It is certainly not unknown for MSS to disappear. Some non-fiction writers I know have sent their books out to twenty or more publishers before anyone nibbled. Make up your mind that this inefficient approach is not for you.

I appreciate that first-time authors may lack the confidence to make such an early approach to a publisher. They may be unsure of the quantity or quality of their material. They may be doubtful of their writing skills. Clearly, writers should never contract to write a book which they may be unable to deliver. To such writers, I recommend that they do only sufficient work on the book to reassure themselves, then they look for a publisher.

I have already said that one of the great advantages of the non-fiction book is the relative ease with which a first-time author can get a contract in advance. Always presuming that your idea for the book is sound and your sales strategy sensible, you too can achieve this great advantage.

A prior contract brings many benefits and should be the aim of every non-fiction writer.

Some of these benefits are:

(a) The publisher is committing himself to publishing your book.

(b) The publisher will agree the length of the book in advance.

(c) The publisher will agree the style and the contents of the book.

(d) There will be professional editorial support during the writing of the book.

(e) There will normally be an agreed advance on royalties to be paid as soon as the contract is signed.

Some of the disadvantages of writing without a prior contract are:

(a) After a great deal of work, the book may prove to be un-saleable.

(b) The publisher approached may already have such a book lined up.

(c) The publisher may not consider unsolicited material.

(d) The book may be totally unsuitable in length.

(e) The approach to the subject may be quite wrong from a sales point of view.

Which publisher?

It is very helpful to know a little of the mechanics of publishing before you approach a publisher. The ideal book on this subject is *An author's guide to publishing* by Michael Legat, published by Hale. Michael has been publisher and author and knows both sides of the coin intimately.

Selecting a publisher is always a speculative venture. As in every business, there are the good, the bad and the indifferent. Large publishing houses may be more professional, but they may be more detached. Small publishers may be able to give you more personal attention, but they may lack the publicity and sales back-up.

I have never worked with a small publisher, but that does not mean I would never do so. I have found the big publishers with whom I have worked a very mixed bag. Some have been painstakingly helpful and a pleasure to work with. Others have ignored vital correspondence and caused such problems that I have had to enlist the help of The Society of Authors to stimulate them into a professional attitude.

If I were starting from scratch today, I would draw up a list of possibles from the major publishers and start at the top, working down until someone showed interest.

Your list can be drawn up from a number of sources. *The Writer's Handbook* and *The Writers' & Artists' Year Book* give the details of publishers and the kind of books they publish. The former is more detailed and also indicates those publishers which do not accept unsolicited material.

Your local library can be a useful guide. Look for books similar to the one you plan. Make sure that they are fairly recent, for publishers' needs change quickly, particularly in these days of takeovers and mergers.

Check books for subject matter, style and approximate length. If you are writing a children's book, check the age group.

Many books run in series, this one for example. If you could adapt your idea to a current series, it would be a good approach.

As always, the librarian can be an invaluable source of information and is well worth approaching with an outline of what you have in mind.

When you have drawn up your list of preferred publishers, you may like to write to some of them for their current book lists. They will send these to you gladly and these will give you the up-to-date details of what they are publishing. If, however, you are reasonably happy with your list you may well prefer to go ahead and make an approach.

Many writers believe that those publishers who state they do not accept unsolicited work are presenting closed doors to the newcomer. This is not the case. The publisher may not accept MSS, but that does not mean that he will reject a query letter.

The query letter

The query letter is of vital importance. It is the bait which you are dangling in front of the publisher and the sole evidence of the merit of your proposal. It must give the essentials, without being too long or verbose. It must paint your proposals in attractive, but not unrealistic colours.

I have phoned publishers, asking for the person dealing with the type of book I have in mind, and putting my initial proposition to them over the phone. It has worked well. However, I realize that most first-time authors would be unhappy with this direct approach and, for them, the carefully worded query letter is the right course.

In your query letter you must state your proposed subject and your qualifications for writing about it, if any. Give brief information on your track-record, particularly if you have had articles on the subject published. You should give the publisher a brief outline of any information you may have on the public interest in your subject. It is helpful, but not essential, to give an approximate length. If your book requires illustration, you should mention the availability of any photographs or other illustrations.

Magazine articles have considerable value at this point. It is a shrewd technique to write a few articles during your research period to back up your sales strategy. Even if they have been accepted but not yet published, it is still very useful to quote them.

Offer to send tear-sheets or photocopies of articles, if the publisher would like to see them. The articles perform several functions. They establish your credibility as a writer. In other words, the publisher can see that you can actually write. They will indicate to the publisher that there is an interest in the subject and, if the magazines are varied in their type of readership, that the interest is wide.

Always type your letter neatly on A4 paper, using a good black ribbon, and enclose an SAE for the reply.

If the publisher is interested, the most likely response will be a request to see a synopsis and a sample chapter or two. He may ask for an outline, not a synopsis. The two terms cause confusion and there is no clear differentiation between them. Most British writers consider an outline to be a brief summary and a synopsis to be longer and broken down into chapters. In America, the tendency seems to be the other way round. The main point is to ensure that you and the publisher are talking about the same thing. If you have any real doubts, phone and ask.

The synopsis

The synopsis must be very carefully thought out. It is important that you should have a fairly clear idea of it before writing the query letter. This enables you to get the synopsis off to the publisher while it is still fresh in his mind. It also creates a good impression.

You are not committing yourself irrevocably to the synopsis. It is provisional and flexible. It is a skeleton which enables the publisher to make up his mind and possibly offer suggestions.

The synopsis should be laid out neatly, again using A4 paper. Type on one side of the paper only. I always double-space mine and leave generous margins as for MSS. This allows the publisher to make alterations and comments. If possible, you should number and title the chapters, putting them in a reasonably logical order. Under each chapter, you should give the salient points to be covered, using a few words for each point. Obviously, you must keep a copy of the synopsis for yourself.

If the publisher is still interested, you may be asked to clarify a few more points or you may be asked to go for a chat. When you go, have a note of any queries you may have and take your copy of the synopsis with you.

You may see the publisher's editor or an editorial director. Listen carefully to all suggestions. Make a note of them, even if you disagree. Don't be afraid to disagree politely, if you feel strongly about a point.

It can be useful if you have some idea of how you think the completed book will look in format, size and illustration.

Ask your questions of the publisher. Be prepared to take ideas away and consider them, rather than give snap decisions which you may regret. It is from this interview that the contract may be given, after due consideration by the publisher.

Rejection

Every writer hates rejections. You must expect them from time to time, particularly in the field of books. There can be many reasons for the rejection. Perhaps you have a good idea which you are perfectly capable of developing, but it would not fit in with the publisher's current lists. It could clash with a very similar book already on the publisher's stocks. I once had a book proposal rejected because it would have been heavily illustrated and the publishers considered it too expensive to produce at a competitive price.

Accept your rejections philosophically. Note any comments and move on to the next publisher on your list. The main thing is not to be discouraged. You would be fortunate if your first query letter brought success.

Some authors make multiple submissions to a number of publishers at the same time. I believe there are distinct disadvantages in doing this. For example, you are showing your hand to a number of publishers who are interested in the same field. You may settle for one, but the seed of the idea for your book has been sown in the minds of the others. It could easily result in the publishing of competing works.

In addition, I have an aversion to making tentative offers and then backing out because something better has come along, unless there is a very good reason for so doing. I believe that sending a query letter to one publisher at a time is a straightforward and sound practice.

Alternative forms of publishing

There are other forms of publishing which might come to your attention and which are worthy of comment.

Vanity publishing

So-called vanity publishing thrives on the first-time author who, ignoring all danger signals, is so eager to see his book in print that he will pay sweetly for the privilege.

The publisher usually advertises that he is anxious to contact new authors with a view to publishing their work. You reply and he asks to see your MS. The publisher comments on this and his fulsome praise suggests that it has real merit. Yes, he will publish it, but the writer must make a financial contribution.

The contribution will be considerable and the number of finished books is often small. The publisher shows a handsome profit on the print run and, from then on, usually shows little interest, for he is away looking for fresh prey. The writer is left with a number of bound volumes, probably a larger number of unbound books and a diminished bank account. The last thing these publishers have in mind is getting involved in the selling.

Vanity publishing comes in a number of thinly-veiled guises, but the key indications are usually that the publisher touts for writers and requires substantial payment to publish your work. Don't be tempted.

Self-publishing

Although self-publishing is the choice of a minority, it is growing in popularity. It requires considerable financial commitment, supreme confidence in the success of one's book and liaison with a reliable printer who has book-production experience.

The writer is faced with writing the book, at least some elements of its production and, finally, the daunting task of selling it. The latter is usually the toughest part of the project.

The work in self-publishing can vary with the degree in which the author involves himself in the process. The more he leaves to the printer, the greater the financial outlay.

Detailed guidance on self-publishing is beyond the scope of this book. An excellent book on the subject is *Guide to self-publishing* by Harry Mulholland. It is self-published, of course, by Mulholland-Wirral, The Croft, School Avenue, Little Neston, South Wirral, L64 4BS.

Books can be bulky and heavy. There are many writers, tempted into self-publishing, whose homes are bulging with unsold books. It must be remembered that the cost of self-publishing is considerable and capital tied up in unsold books could be earning healthy dividends elsewhere with no effort at all.

I believe that self-publishing should not be the last resort of the writer who has failed to interest any publisher in his book. It should be reserved for the book which appears to have an assured market and in which the writer is confident that he will make a far bigger profit by self-publishing.

Most dedicated authors want to write, not to sell books, and the pain and pleasure of both should be weighed up before committing oneself to self-publishing.

Sponsored books

There is a growing number of businesses which sponsor books. You will see examples in most of the large supermarket chain stores. The stores subsidise or completely finance the publication and then often sell it through their own outlets. Those printed under their own name are exclusive to the sponsor, but other sponsored books often have other trade outlets.

Usually, the publisher comes up with the idea for a book and then offers it to a potential sponsor. However, there is an increasing trend for sponsors to make the approach to a number of publishers simultaneously, resulting in some hard bargaining.

Although some established authors approach sponsors with ideas, particularly if they have already written books for them, most publishers make their own choice of authors. Occasionally, sponsors not only come up with the idea, but also suggest an author.

The publishers get about the same amount of unsolicited material as other conventional publishers, but they regard approaches more favourably if the author has a possible sponsor already lined up.

The authors are usually paid royalties in the normal way, but there are occasions when they are offered lump sums, particularly if the book is a short one.

One of the benefits of sponsored books is that they can be produced to a high quality because of the advantage of their guaranteed sales. In addition, the publisher is spared the usual haggling for book club and other cut-price deals.

The author must expect to write to at least some of the requirements of the sponsor, but the publisher does retain most of the editorial control.

Sponsored books are an interesting and developing field which is worth considering for the established writer, but it is not really a market for the beginner.

Packaging

The packagers are a growing breed in the publishing world. Packagers are entrepreneurs who bring together the saleable idea, the publisher, the printer, the writer and, where appropriate, the illustrator.

The author is usually paid a lump sump rather than royalties. Packagers work to very tight schedules with inflexible deadlines. They often rely on fast turnovers and relatively small profit margins.

The packager would normally approach the writer and would be looking for someone who is highly experienced, very professional and capable of writing to order and delivering on time. Packaging is definitely not a field for the beginner.

Most writers use the normal publishers and steer clear of the less conventional. One reason may be that they don't really understand the complexities of packaging, sponsorship and self-publishing. I have never been tempted to move into these fields until recently, but, if negotiations succeed, my next book may be a venture in sponsored self-publishing. In this case, a sponsor with established sales outlets would finance the book which I might publish, retaining a small run of books for myself.

Alternatively, I might settle for straight sponsorship and offer it to a publisher specialising in the sponsoring field. In this case it would earn less money for me, but would require no capital investment with its inherent risk. I could concentrate on writing rather than selling and it would give me a toe in the door of a completely new field for me – a field with considerable potentials.

So, you can see that permutations are possible in this complex world of publishing, but only for the established writer.

Chapter Three

The contract

Many writers seem to be overawed by publishers. Certainly this applies to most first-time authors and some established ones as well. Contracts are often regarded with gratitude rather than with a healthy critical eye. An advance on royalties, the largest single sum that many new authors have ever received for a piece of writing, is often accepted almost cap-in-hand.

Publishers are, in fact, entirely dependent on their authors for survival and it is far from being a case of beggars and choosers.

Most new authors are so overjoyed at receiving that coveted contract that they sign it without query. Indeed, they do so with almost indecent haste, prompted by the fear that the publisher might change his mind.

Negotiating the contract

It is important to understand that the contract which is sent to you is a draft and is not inflexible. It is drafted to meet the best interests of the publisher, but this does not imply that it is essentially unfair or against the writer's interests.

Selling your writing is like selling any other commodity. The seller hopes for a good or at least a fair price. The buyer is probably prepared to pay a fair price, but always hopes for a bargain.

Before drafting a contract the publisher will offer you an

advance and specify the royalty percentages he will pay you. Thus, the main terms will already have been agreed. Ideally, negotiations should be settled before the contract is drafted, but amendments can be made up to the time of signing.

The contract should be subject to negotiation and mutual agreement. The publisher wants your work because he sees it as a profitable transaction. In drafting a contract, time and money have already been invested in the venture. The writer need never fear that asking a publisher to consider an amendment to a contract will bring about cancellation of the offer. The worst that will happen will be a refusal to amend or possibly an offer to negotiate. If you have professional advisers, they will handle these aspects for you, or at least will comment on the draft contract.

All authors should read their contracts carefully, but this is particularly important for new authors. If there are clauses that are difficult to understand, phone the publisher and ask for an explanation. You will not be refused help.

Professional guidance

If you have an agent, this chapter is not for you. Your agent will vet and negotiate the terms of the contract for you. As this is unlikely in the early days, you will have to look elsewhere if you feel the need for professional support.

The Society of Authors will appraise contracts for its members. Although the normal requirement for membership is to have had a full-length book published, The Society recognises the problems new authors have with contracts. It will accept the offer of a contract for a full-length book as sufficient qualification for membership. In this way you can join The Society and have your contract vetted at the same time.

I have used The Society's services on a number of contract matters and have always been well satisfied with its professional advice.

Minimum Terms Agreement

The Society, together with the Writers' Guild, has drawn up a Minimum Terms Agreement (MTA) to improve the standard contract between author and publisher. The two organisations have successfully negotiated agreements with several leading publishers along the lines of the MTA. These agreements are intended to be phrased in understandable language and to provide higher royalties, better protection for authors and all-round improvement on most standard contracts. There is, however, provision for authors to negotiate better terms in each case, if they are able to do so.

Contract details

Although contracts vary considerably in detail, the salient points of those offered by the major publishers tend to follow very similar lines. Because of the variations, it is only possible to generalise and to give broad guidance on some of those main points.

The contract lays down the obligations of both publisher and author in the production of the book. It states the title or provisional title and gives the book's approximate length in words.

Delivery date
The date for delivery of the MS is stated. This, of course, will have been agreed already. It is essential that this date should be well within the author's capabilities, bearing in mind other commitments and unforeseen eventualities. Don't be afraid of insisting on a later date. The publisher would prefer that to a hold-up or a rushed second-rate job. If, as the writing of the book proceeds, you find that you may be unable to meet the date, inform the publisher as early as possible.

Amendments

The publisher may want changes in the MS. For example, he may feel that there would be legal hazards in publishing it as it stands. There could be a wide variety of reasons for this. For example, it might be libellous, obscene, blasphemous or could infringe another's copyright. The contract provides for the publisher to have the author make any amendments deemed necessary.

Amendments asked for by the publisher are intended to be constructive. They will include suggestions for the condensing or expanding of specific aspects, either for change of emphasis or improved clarity.

From my experience, the advice and suggestions of a good editor are invaluable and have invariably improved my books.

However strongly you may feel about it, you will have contracted to amend it and failure to do so could end with the cancellation of the contract and the book being dropped.

The rights

The rights of publication are defined. The copyright should remain with the author, the publisher being given a licence which grants the specified rights and territories in which he may sell the book. Any contract which requires the author to give up his rights must be regarded with the gravest suspicion.

The publisher effectively buys the rights for the full term of copyright, namely, until fifty years after the author's death, as long as the book remains in print in any edition. However, The Society of Authors and the Writers' Guild are pressing for the duration of the licence to be reduced to ten years.

Competing works

It is normal for the author to agree not to write a work for another publisher which competes with the one which is the subject of the contract. However, it may be that you only write on one subject, say cooking. Such a clause would make it very difficult for you to earn a living. Clearly, a tighter definition of what is considered competitive is necessary and this must be agreed before signing the contract.

There is nothing to stop your writing similar books for the same publisher. Indeed, if he is a good publisher there is every incentive for you to do so.

Publication

The publisher agrees the date by which the book will be published. This is usually within twelve months of the delivery of the MS.

The author agrees that the publisher shall have full control of the publication of the work, its paper, printing, binding, jacket, price and the associated publicity.

In practice, the author's suggestions, particularly on the jacket and the jacket 'blurb' etc, may not be unwelcome. In many cases, the author is invited to write the blurb.

Royalties

The royalties paid are usually based on an agreed percentage of the UK retail price of the book. If there are hardback and paperback editions, the royalty rates for both will be quoted. The royalty payments are somewhat complex and usually there are higher percentages as the number of books sold increases. For example, it might be 10% up to 5,000 copies, after which the rate might increase to $12\frac{1}{2}$%.

Export sales have different royalty terms and, on occasions, export sale prices can be extraordinarily low, giving the author almost derisory royalties.

Advances

The publisher will state his offer of an advance on royalties. This will have been agreed already. The advance will usually be paid about one-third on signing the contract, one-third on delivery of the MS and one-third on publication. The dates on which future royalty payments will be made will also be stated; usually this will be twice a year.

The advances on royalties must be earned by future book sales before any further payments are made, but a good advance is always worth pressing for.

If there is a subject about which new authors are disinclined to argue, it must be the advance. Unfortunately, they have no experience on which to base their appraisal of the offer, but increases on the initial offer can frequently be negotiated.

Publishers vary in their yardstick for advances on royalties. It is normally based on the earnings from the first print run. You should ask your publisher how many books he proposes to print in the first run and their cover price. From this you can estimate your royalty earnings from this run. An advance of two-thirds of the first print run's royalty potential is a reasonable expectation.

One point should be stressed. A proportion of the advance is usually paid on delivery of the MS. The author should be wary if the clause reads 'to be paid on acceptance of the MS', which would give the publisher a loop-hole through which to escape from the contract, should he wish to do so.

The Society of Authors warns its members that they should check that there is a firm and unconditional commitment by the publisher to publish the book. The onus is on the publisher to satisfy himself that writing the book satisfactorily is within the author's capabilities. Should the book turn out to be a bad one, despite editing and amendments, the publisher cannot be legally bound to publish. However, failure to do so would be interpreted as a breach of contract.

Occasionally, authors are offered lump sums in full payment, rather than royalties. This is generally considered to be a bad practice and to be avoided.

Subsidiary rights

The contract will probably quote the subsidiary rights granted to the publisher. These may include the sale of paperback rights to another publisher, book club rights and a whole range of apparently unlikely prospects, including TV, film, braille and even strip-cartoon rights. You will be paid an agreed percentage of the publisher's receipts or profits from such sales.

Warranty
The author gives a warranty that the work is his own property and that he has the power to sign the contract. He states that nothing in the book is libellous or otherwise likely to attract legal action. He also agrees to indemnify the publisher against such action.

Libel
The risk of libel particularly applies to biographies, exposés and other works concerning the behaviour or character of others. It is a complex area and can also be a very costly one. Current court awards in libel cases are often hundreds of thousands of pounds and even more. It is self-evident that such a risk is not worth taking.

It is true that authors can insure themselves against claims for libel, but the premiums are expensive. For most of us, taking care to avoid such trouble is the best course.

Illustrations
The contract often makes the author responsible for the cost of illustrations. This can be very expensive, particularly for fully illustrated books in colour. The author would be wise to try to get the publisher to meet, or at least share, the cost.

It is possible that the publisher will agree to pay up to an agreed sum, but if the author insists on more lavish illustration it will be at his own expense.

Even if the author is to be responsible for all illustrations, it is often possible to arrange for the publisher to meet the cost initially and then deduct the sum from future royalties.

Index
If the publisher decides that an index is necessary, the contract will probably state that this will be at the author's expense. It is

up to the author to decide if he will index the book himself or employ a professional indexer. Alternatively, the publisher can arrange the indexing and charge the cost to the author.

Proofs

The author agrees to read the proofs of the work, to correct any errors and return them to the publisher within a stated time, probably 2–3 weeks.

The contract will normally state that the cost of amending the errors over, say, 10% of the cost of typesetting, will be paid by the author. Printers' errors are excluded. As typesetting corrections can be very expensive, it provides a high incentive for the author to edit his MS very carefully before submission.

Revision

The author usually agrees to revise the book, if necessary, in order to keep it up-to-date.

Quoted material

If the book includes quoted copyright material, it is the author's responsibility to obtain permission to use it and, usually, to pay for any cost for its use. This permission should always be obtained in writing from the publisher of the material, in plenty of time.

Free copies

The publisher agrees to provide the author with a stated number of free copies of the book and further copies of future editions. Some publishers are generous and others are parsimonious. Authors are normally allowed to purchase further copies for their own use at trade price.

Sales promotion

The author usually agrees to be available for the promotion of the book at the time of publication. This does not mean that the author must be at the publisher's beck and call for all manner of public appearances. Usually, the publisher will ask the author if he is available for any particular promotion which is planned.

This type of publicity can be very demanding, particularly if it includes radio and TV broadcasts. You should decide in advance whether you want to be so deeply involved and let your publisher know accordingly.

Remainders
Should the book's sales fail to fulfil expectations, the publisher may decide to sell off the remaining copies at a greatly reduced price. In the contract, the publisher usually states the minimum time lapse before he will remainder the books, perhaps one or two years after publication. The author should ensure that it is agreed that he will be offered the opportunity to buy any remaindered copies at the reduced price.

This is only a brief summary of some points in a fairly lengthy legal document, possibly some twelve foolscap pages. Contracts vary considerably in their detail from publisher to publisher, author to author and even book to book. Most of the points mentioned will be developed further in later chapters.

Few authors would profess to be completely conversant with the diversity of publishing contracts. Those who have no access to professional advice would be well-advised to read the contract most carefully. An excellent booklet entitled *Publishing Contracts* is available free to members from The Society of Authors. Non-members may obtain copies, currently priced at £1.50, post free. This guide can be valuable when appraising a new contract.

Once you are reasonably satisfied, sign the contract and return it to the publisher. You should receive your own copy, signed by the publishers, in due course. Check it and file it carefully.

Subsequent contracts will seem easier to understand and, as confidence grows, you may well be able to negotiate better deals.

Chapter Four

Research

The ability to research effectively is vital for the successful non-fiction writer and it is a skill which must be developed.

There can be very few non-fiction books which are written without reference to outside sources for at least some of their material. Obviously, there are books which need little research beyond the personal knowledge or experience of the writer. Others may require years of literary research, extensive travelling and many in-depth interviews.

Even autobiographies usually need some research, particularly if they refer to national events, for most of us have fickle memories.

Most of the world's total knowledge is recorded somewhere and the sound researcher has a good idea how to find it. Note that I did not say *where* to find it, for even a professional researcher would be unable to say, without reference, precisely where more than a tiny percentage of material could be found.

The secret is *how* to find it – which reference book to reach for – which learned association to contact – which expert to consult. This is the knowledge which is the basis of the effective researcher's skills. It is knowledge which is difficult to acquire. It is expensive knowledge to buy if you wish to use the professional researcher's services, and rightly so.

Fortunately, the non-fiction author usually has little need for such comprehensive knowledge, but can afford to specialise and gradually build up a research expertise in limited subjects. In addition, he must have a good idea where to find the signposts which will lead to material in new areas. Inevitably, the average author will be much slower than the professional researcher, but the paths and stepping-stones are there and he should be able to find most of them eventually.

There is no better book on the subject than *Research for writers* by Ann Hoffmann, published by A & C Black. Ann is a professional researcher of great experience and also the author of a number of non-fiction books. Her book is revised regularly. In it she confirms: 'While the specialist must know his pet subject inside out, there is no question but that for the general writer the knowledge of *where to go* to find what he needs is of the greater value.' Her book tells its readers precisely how to do so.

The initial steps

Few writers take up a subject from scratch. As most of us write about subjects which appeal to us, it is almost certain that you will have some knowledge of the subject. If you gather together this knowledge, probably you will be surprised to find how much you know already.

A sound first step is to consult a good encyclopedia, either your own or in your public library. In addition to the information on the subject, there will often be a bibliography suggesting further reading.

The ASLIB *Directory of Information Sources in the UK* is a valuable tool for the researcher. It is a comprehensive signpost to a wide variety of sources of information and is published by the Association of Special Libraries and Information Bureaux. It should be available in your central library.

I find that library copies are often out of date. If your library has an old edition, it is always worthwhile asking for it to be replaced.

Libraries

Dewey Decimal System

It is sensible and a time-saver to become familiar with the Dewey Decimal Filing System under which British public libraries classify their books.

It divides the subjects into ten main numerical divisions from 000 to 900. From these general classes, subdivisions lead to narrower classifications until decimal figures are used to identify specialised subjects.

The main divisions are:

000	Generalities
100	Philosophy and related disciplines
200	Religion
300	Social Sciences
400	Language
500	Pure sciences
600	Technology (applied science)
700	The arts, recreation
800	Literature
900	General geography and history

Suppose the subject of your research was the cultivation of roses. You would first go to 600 – Technology. Garden crops are found in the sub-division 635. Flowers and ornamental plants are under 635.9. Individual plants come under 635.93 and this is further sub-divided by botanical families, genera and species to 635.933. Finally, you would arrive at the cultivation of roses under 635.93372.

This may seem clumsy and over elaborate, but it is an excellent system which works well. In practice, public libraries rarely use more than three decimal places, although, in theory, there is no limit.

Dewey is not used in every library and you may occasionally come across other systems in, for example, some university libraries.

Local libraries
The British lending and reference libraries are an excellent source, although often painfully slow in obtaining books which are not held locally. Of course, they vary in their size and service. My own library is tiny and open only three days a week, but the staff is still most helpful.

Librarians are usually very knowledgeable and eager to help. If you tell the librarian of your particular needs, you will be offered advice on suitable source books. By librarian I mean professional librarian and these are not normally to be found in small local libraries. You may well have to go to your central library to enlist their expertise.

The assistance you will receive varies. It can include the selection of appropriate books, even flagged at the point of your interest. Such help can be time-saving and invaluable.

Copyright libraries
The copyright libraries are very comprehensive storehouses of written knowledge. They are located in London, Cambridge, Oxford, Edinburgh and Aberystwyth. Admission is by reader's ticket only and, although day tickets can be obtained, it is wise to apply for a ticket in advance.

Under the Copyright Act, 1911, every publisher must send a free copy to the British Library of every book published. The other copyright libraries must be supplied with copies if they make application for them.

British Library
Located in the British Museum, the British Library is considered to be the finest in the world. It has a vast collection of books, maps, manuscripts and other publications.

The British Library has an associated newspaper library situated at Colindale. Admission here is also by reader's ticket.

The library is in great demand by students, researchers and others. Access to the books is restricted to those who are unable to obtain their information elsewhere. You must satisfy this condition if you apply for a reader's ticket.

Relatively few books are readily accessible on open shelves and most books must be applied for. This entails finding the catalogue number of the books you require, using the huge catalogues available. You complete an application form and hand it in to the central desk and then await delivery of your books. This can take hours and, in the case of books which are stored outside the library building, they may not arrive until the next day.

It is a good idea to order your books in advance. For this you will require a supply of application forms, picked up on a previous visit to the library. The catalogue numbers of your books can be obtained from the British Library catalogue, a copy of which is kept in most central libraries. As these copies are in a greatly reduced format, most people will find they need a magnifying glass to read them.

Fill in the forms, giving the details of the books you require and state the date when you are attending. Post to the British Library, giving several days' notice.

Special libraries
There are many libraries which are devoted to one subject, medicine, for example. Their great advantage is that, not only are you undistracted by other subjects but you can soon become conversant with their layout and contents and, even more important, their staff know their library intimately. The ASLIB Directory lists these libraries.

Other sources

Public Relations Officers can be helpful. Although some PROs seem to be too busy to answer specific questions, they will usually send out information packs. They are employed by most large industries, government departments and many other bodies.

For foreign material, you will find that embassies, high commissions, tourist boards and foreign libraries can be useful sources of information. Some, however, may send irrelevant material or ignore the enquiry altogether.

Those who specialise will build up contacts and sources of information which deal with their speciality. This personal knowledge is invaluable and must be filed carefully for future use.

Field research

Although some writers can and do write about places they have never seen and do so with a surprisingly intimate style, this can only be a second best. It is desirable, and in some cases essential, for some material to be obtained first hand on location. For example, if you were writing a book on the history, folklore and topography of a Hebridean island, it would be impossible to do justice to it merely through the eyes of others. You would need to go there, see for yourself, talk to people, soak up the atmosphere and possibly take photographs.

Before such trips, it is essential to do as much armchair research as possible in advance. In this way, you should know where to go to discover rich material, whom to talk to and many other points which will save time. Even the time of the year to go could be vital.

You must make every effort to ensure that your facts are accurate. This is not always easy, for reference books often copy each other and perpetuate mistakes. Too many books are mere re-hashes of the work of others. The way out of this regurgitation of stale and often incorrect material lies in intelligent and original research. If possible, go back to the original source or, at least, try to test the validity of your statements.

Many readers, who would never dream of writing to a publisher to say they have enjoyed a book, can't wait to write and pour ridicule on some minor error. Be warned. Check and double-check your facts.

You should also check areas which may have been subject to change, in order to bring up to date the material already gathered.

I remember going to a beautiful and remote bay in Scotland to take photographs and do some research. I was shocked to find a new village of workmen's huts and a half-built oil-rig dominating the landscape. Had I written from memory, I would have been utterly wrong, possibly luring readers to a false paradise.

Time is always precious, but do leave sufficient for the unexpected. Sometimes on location, you will hear of a fascinating subject of which you were unaware and which just begs to be investigated. Few things can be more frustrating than having to abandon the idea because of lack of time.

If you are taking photographs, you will have to allow for bad weather. Hanging around on trips can be an expensive business. I get round this on many occasions in UK by using a trailer caravan. It is much cheaper than hotels. It gives me privacy and peace to get on with some writing during any delays. It also gives me the flexibility of coming and going as I please.

Field research can include not merely talking to people, but also conducting structured interviews. As this can be an important part of research it is dealt with in a separate chapter.

Research may be fascinating, but is also time-consuming. The wise author, researching for his book, must often look at the economics of his research. For example, would it be worth the time and money to travel several hundred miles to interview someone whose comments would occupy no more than a paragraph or two in the book? Of course, it might be worth it. These paragraphs might be vital if they were the previously unpublished comments of a witness in a murder case, the history of which is the subject of your book.

You need enough research to produce your book, plus something in hand. Digging too deeply becomes a superfluous exercise and interferes with your prime purpose of writing.

In time, most writers develop their research skills to a high level. They learn to find their way round the standard sources of material, plus those which specialise in their own particular needs. The good researcher acquires an intuitive feel for discarding the dross, identifying the semi-precious and ferreting out the true jewels.

Obviously, all your research material must be filed in an efficient manner which allows easy retrieval. Filing systems will be covered in the chapter on the business side of writing.

Chapter Five

Interviewing

The subject of interviewing for research was covered in some depth in my book, *The Way To Write Magazine Articles*. The points which were made are no less valid when considering research for books, although it inevitably means some repetition.

In magazine articles, the interview is quite often the peg on which the piece hangs. This rarely happens in a book. Even a biography which includes lengthy interviews with the subject would probably be a blend of fact, comment and interviews with others.

Although interviewing may only be a small facet of a book, it can be very important. For this reason, every non-fiction writer should know how to conduct an effective interview and how to use the material gained to best advantage.

I accept that some writers hate interviews and will avoid them at all costs. If they are adamant about this, they could severely restrict the range of books they write. This is up to the individual. However much we may bow to the whims of our publisher and agent, the writer can at least decide which books he will or will not write.

I enjoy interviews. Some, of course, are more enjoyable than others. Interviews take us away from the dust of books and old manuscripts and into the world of real, three-dimensional people. We ask questions and we get answers – sometimes surprising answers. We may come away with an abundance of material or, perhaps, with very little. Rarely will we come away empty-handed and we are always wiser from the experience.

Interviews for book research tend to fall into two main categories. There is the specialist interview, where the interviewee specialises in a subject and you need to tap his knowledge. Usually, this knowledge will be factual and less likely to have many sensitive aspects of a personal nature. The other is the more personal interview about matters which may have emotional overtones. The former is usually straightforward. The latter can call for considerable interviewing skill for the best results. The more sensitive the area concerned, the more adept the interviewer should be.

The tools of the interview

It is vital that all material which surfaces in an interview must be recorded for possible use. It is a complete waste of time to come away from an interview with a few scraps of notes and your head buzzing with fascinating details, to find later that only half of it can be remembered.

I use a tape-recorder frequently. I always ask permission to use it, but very few people seem to object to it. Even those who appear uneasy at first soon relax and forget about it.

My model is a Philips Micro-cassette recorder. It is pocket-size, lightweight and effective. The only snag with these small models is the relatively short duration of the tapes. The Philips model gives just 30 minutes on each side.

Test tape-recorders immediately prior to use. Always carry spare batteries and tapes. With 30-minute tapes, keep a wary eye on the passage of time, as it can fly during a fascinating interview. Change tapes in plenty of time, say after 25 minutes. I use a wrist-watch which has a stop-watch facility.

Always carry a notebook. Subjects may refuse to allow a tape-recorder and, in any case, written notes can be invaluable for supplementing the recording. The correct spelling of names and difficult words should always be printed in full and all salient points should be noted. Bear in mind that tape-recorders and their tapes are not infallible and back-up notes could prove to be vital.

I use a spiral-backed shorthand notebook. It is fairly small and folds flat.

I try to write my notes by keeping the notebook in the periphery of my vision while maintaining eye-contact with the subject. Eye-contact is important, not only for adequate communication, but also to measure the subject's reactions to questions and revelations, particularly when discussing sensitive matters.

Pens have a habit of running out at inconvenient times, so always carry several spares.

Before leaving for the interview, make sure you have a note of the subject's name, address and phone number. The latter can be invaluable if you can't find the house, particularly in rural areas. It is also essential in case you are inadvertently held up and late for the appointment.

It is a good idea to have a tick-sheet of all the essentials you need to carry, to ensure that nothing is left behind.

Interviewing the expert

I use the term expert loosely. It covers anyone who has specialist knowledge or skills which you need to research for your book.

It is important to obtain as much background information in advance as possible. It enables you to ask the right questions, understand the answers and establish your professionalism. Experts are usually busy people and it would be very unprofessional to take up such a person's valuable time without the courtesy of some preparation. It would also be wrong to expect such an expert to go back to simple basics, although, in practice, he may well do so.

For example, if you were writing a book on the fashionable subject of environmental pollution, you would probably want to talk to experts on acid-rain, nitrogen in rivers, waste disposal, etc. All these subjects could be fairly easily researched in advance.

If, for any reason, you are unable to research the background in advance, then you should say so and apologise. Conversely, you should never pretend to more knowledge than you have. Inevitably, you will be unmasked.

Obviously, there can be sensitive areas when interviewing experts. Considering your environmental book, you may want to interview a farmer who uses heavy dressings of nitrogenous fertilisers on his land or an industrialist who is aware that his factory is visibly polluting a river. They can be expected to be cautious in their replies, colouring them to justify their activities.

To balance the picture you might interview a householder living in the shadow of a nuclear reactor or a chemical plant. He will probably be anxious, aggrieved or both. He may try to manipulate you, slanting the answers to help his cause. In each case, the writer must handle the interview with diplomacy and tact, trying to recognize the position of each interviewee and adopting an objective point of view.

Sensitive interviews

There are some interviews whose sensitivity is self-evident. An example might be the study of homeless children in London. You would need to roam the streets and visit day-shelters and hostels.

To complete the picture you would need to discover the whereabouts of the parents and interview them also. You could only do this by winning the youngsters' confidence and that would only be possible if you were a good interviewer.

I have chosen a particularly difficult subject as an example because of the special problems it would create. There would be the difficulty or impossibility of making appointments and the near impossibility of getting the subjects away from their group. There would be the suspicion you would arouse and the real probability that the subject, hoping for a reward, would colour the answers in a way which he or she felt you wanted.

The basics of effective interviewing

Always make a prior appointment, if possible. Write or phone, giving a brief outline of what you are doing and why you want the subject's assistance. If writing, always enclose a SAE.

Be punctual for the appointment. Try to get the measure of the subject. Is he a busy man from whom you will have to wring out precious facts against the clock? He may, for example, say, 'I'm sorry, but I can only give you twenty minutes.' In such cases keep the preamble to the minimum required by good manners and go straight into the questions. Don't remind him when the twenty minutes are up. It may have been no more than a pose or a let-out and he may find that he is enjoying the interview more than he expected.

In other cases, and particularly in sensitive interviews, it is wise to start in a low key – more a chat than an interview. Use easy, unstressful questions at the beginning, giving the subject time to relax, get to know you and warm up.

Interviews for research must have direction. You have neither the time nor the motivation for the aimless conversation. You must take charge if you are going to get your value from the interview. After the low key introduction, you must be purposeful.

From the background research, you should note all the questions you wish to ask, together with possible follow-up questions, depending on the answers received.

Always try to keep time in hand for the exploration of unexpected revelations. These may be very important and time-consuming.

Skilled interviewers get an intuitive feel for their relationship with the subject. I often think of research interviewers as being rather like well-trained sheepdogs. They move slowly and cautiously. They know when to remain still – alert, attentive, listening. They know when to advance a little. They know when to back off if their subject shows anxiety or panic and they let them relax a little. Yet all the time they have their goal in mind – the area towards which they are imperceptibly guiding their subject.

Once they have achieved their goal, like the good sheep-dog, they take the pressure off and everyone relaxes. Again, the good interviewer ends on a low key and tries to ensure that, on reflection, the subject feels that the interview was a pleasant experience.

Listening is a skill. Too many of us want to talk, rather than listen. Many interviewers allow their attention to wander during the boring parts, only coming alert when an interesting point is reached. This boredom is usually obvious.

I remember being told about an old lady who thanked the interviewer when he left. She apologised for her story being so boring, but she said that she did appreciate that the interviewer had been clever enough to manage to yawn with his mouth closed.

When you listen, you must pay attention, not merely to the words, but also to the tone of voice, the facial expressions, the tensions in the body and the nervous hand movements. These signs are called, very aptly, body language.

It is a language which speaks clearly to the skilled interviewer. It can tell him when the interview is moving towards a change in emotional field. The subject may register relief at escaping from an uncomfortable line of questioning; he may become anxious, angry, exhilarated or unhappy. Remember, these emotions are not essentially felt towards the interviewer, but are possibly inspired by the memories which have been invoked. However, such emotions can still break through into the interviewing relationship and be projected on to the interviewer. The skill lies in knowing how to handle these situations, limiting distress to the subject, yet achieving success in obtaining the required material.

On leaving the interview, it is important to review the material as soon as possible. I usually do this in the car. I read my notes, amplifying them where necessary while the facts are still fresh in my mind.

A question I am often asked is whether the subject should be entitled to see the typescript of the interview before it goes to the publisher. Writers have differing opinions about this. If it is an interview that is rich in factual information, it would be wise to ensure that your interpretation of these facts is correct. For other interviews, I am anxious not to get involved in fruitless editing to suit the whim of the interviewee.

At the end of the interview, I always ask if anything has been divulged which the subject would prefer me not to use. If so, I always respect their wish, no matter how valuable I might consider that material.

It is courteous to write to interviewees, thanking them for their contribution to your work. If the contribution is particularly valuable, you may wish to consider an acknowledgement in the book and even, perhaps, a complimentary copy.

Questionnaires

I find questionnaires can be valuable in some circumstances. They are particularly useful when:

1. Specific answers are required to a few straightforward questions.
2. When the interviewee is geographically remote, or when the extent of the material will probably be small relative to the travelling involved.
3. When the subject refuses an interview, but is willing to accept a questionnaire as an alternative.

I used several questionnaires in the research for this book and found them invaluable.

The interview type of questionnaire is aimed specifically at an individual and is not to be confused with the mail-shot type.

When I was researching this book, I sent a typical questionnaire to a publisher of sponsored books. It looked something like this:

1. Who is usually the prime-mover in sponsored publication? Does the sponsor approach the publisher or do publishers come up with good ideas and offer them to potential sponsors?
2. Do authors ever approach sponsors or publishers direct?
3. I would expect publishers to make their own choice of authors for commissions. Is this the case?
4. Do sponsors invariably have the exclusive sales of their books or can publishers use other trade outlets?
5. Does payment to authors follow the usual pattern of royalties or are they ever paid lump sums?
6. Are there any other interesting points in which sponsored publishing differs from the norm?

I always write or phone first, obtaining the subject's agreement before sending a questionnaire. If writing, I always enclose a SAE.

Questionnaires should have precise and carefully thought out questions. The questions should be typed on one side of the paper only, leaving ample space for the reply after each question. I always finish by inviting the subject to add anything which they might feel would be helpful and I leave a generous space for them to do so. Again, I enclose a SAE and I always write and thank them when they return a completed questionnaire.

If your questions require no more than simple answers, then a straightforward letter inviting comment may well be preferable to a more formal questionnaire. It is up to you to judge which is more appropriate.

As in any other form of research, interview material must be factually accurate. In interviewing there is sometimes the temptation for the beginner to accept answers at their face value. They say, 'He told me so himself,' or 'I got it first-hand from a chap who was there', just as if the source were infallible.

Remember that material obtained from interviews can be inaccurate for a variety of reasons. These can be lapses of memory, hearsay information, mere embroidery or downright lies.

Memory can be fickle. The desire to enhance the good parts and play down the bad is a common human trait. In re-telling a story over the years, it changes its colour, perhaps becoming more heroic, more glamorous, less sordid and shameful. Eventually the story-teller almost believes the latest version.

I remember an old lady in her eighties swearing to me that her father had only one brother and no sisters. Yet I knew from indisputable evidence that her father had a sister. She became so agitated that I dropped the question. Later I found that her aunt had given birth to an illegitimate child and, such was the stigma of this in those days, she chose to deny that her aunt had ever existed.

If possible, material should be checked back to root sources. If unconfirmed material is too important to leave out, it should be qualified in some way. For example, you could precede it with 'It is said that . . .'

Another form of inaccuracy can be introduced by the bias of the interviewer. It can be deliberate or unconscious. The choice of questions which are asked can dictate the information received. 'Of course, you do support nuclear disarmament?', for example. A remark of the interviewee which fails to fit in with the writer's theme may be ignored rather than pursued. Later, when the material is being sifted and marshalled, the less scrupulous writer may select only those aspects which fit his preconceived plan for the book.

A great deal depends on the purpose of the book. It would be very unlikely for a whole interview to be reported verbatim and so some selection is inevitable. If your book is to be an accurate representation of facts and opinions, then those for and against must be recorded. If, however, you are writing on a narrow aspect of the subject, then irrelevancies would be deleted.

The best advice I can give is to record as much information as possible and then edit it to meet your needs, but to do so with integrity.

Photography at interviews

It can often be useful to have a photograph of a person you interview. It has particular value if you take it yourself, and, therefore, hold the copyright. You many not even use the photograph in your book, but it could well be an attractive addition to any articles which you may write as a spin-off from the book.

Conventional portrait photography really requires careful lighting and posing, which is rarely practical for the average author. It is usually better to aim for the more casual picture with basic lighting and the minimum of posing.

Always tell the subjects in advance that you would like a few informal photographs. This gives them a chance to refuse or to prepare themselves.

Outdoor shots are more straightforward, but depend on weather conditions. Photographs in the garden can be very attractive.

It is sensible to get some practice in portrait photography by using friends and family. Practise with both natural lighting and flash, in both black and white and colour. I advise the inexperienced photographer against using house-lighting for colour shots, as ordinary colour films are made to suit daylight and/or flash only.

Take plenty of shots; if you are using colour, it is wise to bracket the exposure. (See the chapter on illustrating.)

If the subject is being interviewed because of his or her involvement in some activity, take shots of him or her engaged in it or with some evidence of it in the picture.

Records of interviews

Interviews are usually time-consuming. There is the preparatory research, the correspondence, the travelling, the interview itself and the analysing of the results. It is unwise to scrap all this work once the book is completed, without very careful thought. You may feel that the *essence* of the interview will be in the completed book, but remember that much will have been edited out.

I keep all the written notes and observations made at the interview. I make sure the subject's name, address and phone number are recorded. I run through the tapes, extract all the points which might be of interest in the future and write them down. Very occasionally, I keep the tapes themselves, particularly with interviews which I had overseas. All this material is carefully filed. It may be valuable for articles or even for a future book. If so, it could save a great deal of time and, in some cases, the material could be irreplaceable.

You may well write books without a single interview. They are not essential and, in some cases, would be inappropriate. Yet a fine interview, rich in material, can bring a great deal of satisfaction to a writer. Using quoted speech, it can breathe life into heavy passages, giving a book a new sparkle. It is such interviews that many writers look back on as some of the more memorable features of their writing careers.

Chapter Six

Illustrating the book

The value of illustrations depends largely on the type of non-fiction book you are writing. For some books, illustrations will be vital. Indeed, some are just picture books with the limited text being little more than captions.

A travel book on the author's trip to an unexplored tributary of the Amazon or a remote region of the Himalayas would really require illustrations to succeed. A field guide to edible fungi would not only be incomprehensible, it would also be downright dangerous without illustrations. The step-by-step account of how to build furniture would be virtually useless without pictures or diagrams to clarify it.

Colour illustrations are expensive to print. Black and white photographs are cheaper, but more expensive than black and white line drawings. The publisher must use his judgement and equate the attraction of photographic illustrations against the public's disincentive to purchase the book because of its high price.

It has been said that a picture is worth a thousand words. In hard cash terms, this is usually untrue. I have written a book, illustrated with forty of my own photographs, for which I was paid no extra. It is true that I was paid for the package – words and pictures – but the payment bore no relationship to the amount that would have been paid had the photography been commissioned. However, the pictures would have been so difficult to obtain that no publisher would have been interested in buying the book if I had been unable to supply them.

Some contracts state that you, the author, will be responsible for providing the illustrations. This is not too worrying if you can do so with your own photographs or drawings. If, however, they have to be obtained from an outside source, then it could be very expensive. In which case, it would be wise for the author to try to negotiate for the publisher to pay all or part of the cost. The publisher will usually be reasonable about this. (See Chapter 3 on contracts.)

The availability of suitable illustrations can often tip the balance when a publisher is hesitating over whether to buy a book. For this reason, it is important to make it clear at the outset of negotiations that such illustrations exist.

What is a good illustration?

A good illustration for a book is a clear picture which tells a story, shows or explains something for which words alone are inadequate or, by its eye-catching qualities, makes the reader stop turning the pages in order to study it.

Even relatively poor illustrations can be useful if they are unique and perform one of the above functions, particularly if they are copies of old photographs or engravings, required for historical books.

A book on how the writer bought a Hebridean island and converted an old fish-curing factory into a home could only be illustrated by the author's own step-by-step photographs, however modest they might be.

Photography

With the great advances in modern cameras and films, even photographers with modest skills can turn out publishable material with a little care.

Most photographers use the 35mm SLR (single lens reflex)

camera. It has the advantages of being compact, lightweight and, because it is mass-produced, relatively cheap. It also comes with varying degrees of automation, which does much of the thinking for you. A comprehensive range of interchangeable lenses is available for all but the cheapest models.

Black and white photography has much to recommend it. The film is cheap. It is tolerant of errors in exposure. It has considerable latitude in the darkroom processing stage. It is less expensive to publish and, on that count, could prove more attractive to the publisher.

The film is obtainable in varying speeds, which control the film's sensitivity to light. I do most of my black and white photography with the medium speed Ilford FP4 and, for poor light or action photography, Ilford HP5 or Kodak Tri-X.

It pays to develop your own black and white film, which is a simple process and requires no darkroom. You can then send selected negatives to a processing laboratory for enlargement, if you have no darkroom facilities yourself.

The size the publisher will prefer for publication is 254 x 203 mm (10 x 8 inches) and it should be on a glossy paper. Preference is for borderless prints.

The paper I use for my enlargements for publication is the resin-coated Ilford Multigrade, a paper which gives the photographer great control over contrast and which dries flat, without any tendency to cockle.

The most acceptable colour illustrations are from colour transparencies. Although good quality prints can be used, the results are inferior to those from good transparencies. Generally speaking, publishers prefer transparencies, particularly for books. Colour negative films and the associated processes are constantly improving and prints are slowly finding more favour, particularly with newspapers and some magazines.

The quality of transparencies is more critical than the quality of black and white. Strong, fully saturated colour is demanded and, for this, accurate exposure or even slight under-exposure is required.

When the exposure of a shot is difficult to assess, it is a wise precaution to bracket the exposure. This entails taking a shot at the exposure which you judge to be correct. Then take further exposures a half or a whole stop above and a half or a whole stop below. This is particularly important if you are on location with little chance of repeating the exercise. Remember, film is relatively cheap. Don't be afraid to use it.

The film I use for colour in my 35 mm camera is Kodachrome 64, with the slower speed Kodachrome 25 for specially fine work. For my medium-format 6 cm x 6 cm camera, I use Ektachrome 64 Professional, but Kodachrome 64 Professional is new on the market and is expected to lead the field in this format for the professional.

Film stocks which are described as professional differ from non-professional film and require special care. As films age, their colour response changes. Non-professional film has a built-in tolerance in the expectation that many amateurs will keep them on the shelf or in the camera for some time before they are finally processed. The professional film is already 'ripened' and is in its optimum state for immediate use.

In order to prevent the ripening process continuing in professional film, it should be kept in a refrigerated condition. It should also be processed as soon as possible after exposure.

In practice, all film which is likely to be kept for some time can be usefully refrigerated. However, refrigerated film must be allowed to warm up for about an hour to room temperature before being loaded in the camera, otherwise there could be condensation problems.

Photographic copying

A very easy and cheap way of illustrating a book is by using photographic copies of old prints, engravings and woodcuts etc. These illustrations can be found in old books which are out of copyright. Many are of good quality and reproduce well.

Copying such illustrations is fairly straightforward and not beyond the capabilities of the average amateur photographer. Alternatively, they could be copied professionally.

It is important to satisfy yourself that originals used are really out of copyright. Illustrations in facsimile reproductions of old books should not be copied without reference to the publisher as their copyright is questionable.

Most people have some skills in taking photographs, however basic they may be. Although you may have a fully-automated camera, it is wise to learn as much as you can of manual operation and about your camera in particular. Study the manufacturer's handbook thoroughly. There are more comprehensive books available on most cameras, explaining their function in greater depth.

Camera clubs vary in their fields of interest, but are usually valuable sources of guidance for the novice. Many adult further education colleges run courses for weekends and longer periods. It is important to look for one which meets your interests and is pitched somewhere near your level of skill.

The good photographic illustration is pin sharp in its focusing and not blurred by unsteady handling. It should be correctly exposed and show precisely the subject you intend to portray.

Good composition comes from looking at your work critically. Check that the background and foreground are uncluttered and not distracting. Make sure that there are no amateurish mistakes, like trees appearing to grow from people's heads.

Reading books and even attending courses can only take you so far. You must have plenty of 'hands–on' practice. At the end of the day it comes down to using your camera and being prepared to expend a lot of film.

Black and white is the best film for learning new skills, because it is so cheap, particularly if you process it yourself. Make a note of every shot you take – time of day, shutter speed, aperture, light conditions etc. Only by referring back and comparing results with your notes will you learn where mistakes are made. Believe me, it is nowhere as difficult as it sounds.

Graphics

You may feel that you are no artist and have little drawing talent. This should not discourage you from trying simple illustrations, using the aids which simplify this work.

Straight line drawing is easy, providing angles are correct and line thickness is constant. I use a small and cheap version of the professional draughtsman's drawing board. It is made by Rotring and has a magnetic grip for the paper, a sliding and locking parallel rule and an adjustable associated protractor.

White cartridge paper, card or tracing film should be used. I find Rotring pens excellent, with their interchangeable nibs and large reservoirs, giving lines of consistent thickness throughout.

With a little practice, lettering becomes straightforward using dry transfer lettering such as Letraset.

The drawing should be larger than the intended illustration. I draw mine on A4. For full page illustrations the frame of the drawing should be in the same proportions as the book page. The publisher can tell you the proposed page size.

It is important to remember that the final illustration will probably be greatly reduced from your drawing. Both lettering and lines will also be reduced. You must make allowance for this or you might finish with lettering which is too small and lines which are spidery.

Other sources of illustrations

If your book needs illustrations and you have none of your own and are unable to take them for yourself, then you have to look elsewhere. This means that you have to track down existing pictures or you must have them taken for you. Generally, this will prove expensive and should be carefully considered before embarking on the project.

Commissioning a professional photographer to obtain illustrations can cost several hundreds of pounds a day, plus expenses.

Few authors would agree to provide such illustrations at their own expense.

In cases where such photography appears to be the only solution, close liaison with the publisher is essential. The author should be left in no doubt about the ultimate cost involved before any work is commissioned.

At the time of writing, a new Copyright, Design and Patents Act is about to become law. Under this Act, commissioned photography is no longer the property of the commissioner, but that of the photographer. Photographs commissioned for a book cannot be re-used elsewhere without further fees being due to the photographer.

Many books rely heavily on picture libraries and agencies for their illustrations. Such libraries are stocked with the work of many photographers, often specialists in their field. You pay a reproduction fee for the use of the illustration. The fees vary widely, often linked to the size of the reproduction and the type of publication for which it is intended. A heavily illustrated book using a great deal of material from picture libraries would be very expensive.

Most picture libraries tend to specialise. There are those which cover such subjects as sport, agriculture, crime, space travel, wildlife, marine subjects and very much more. The John Kobal Collection contains only pictures from past films, right back to the early days of the cinema. If you want a still of Charles Laughton as Henry VIII, they will have it. The Mary Evans Picture Library specialises in historical illustrations, mostly prior to 1914. If you want a print of Hogarth's Gin Lane, they can supply it.

The best guide to the picture libraries is *The Picture Researcher's Handbook* by Hilary and Mary Evans and Andra Nelki, published by David & Charles.

If a book is to be illustrated, the expense dictates that the pictures must be carefully selected. Each picture must fulfil its purpose. The number of illustrations will be discussed with the

55

publisher and, ideally, a good range should be taken along for the publisher's selection. This face-to-face discussion is preferable to post and telephone communication, if the publisher agrees.

Even if you are unable to provide the illustrations, the publisher will be pleased to hear of any sources you may know. During your research you may have seen picture credits in books and magazines, the illustrations looking as if they might be suitable for your book. If so, make a note of them for future reference.

Finally, there is a particular satisfaction in writing a book and illustrating it yourself. Don't be too deterred by apparent difficulties. They can usually be overcome.

Chapter Seven

Writing the book

The book framework

Some authors can sit down and write their books as the thoughts flow. Although this may be suitable for fiction, for most non-fiction books it is important to have a preconceived framework or skeleton. Although there are exceptions, it is normally in this way that the progression can be balanced and the book achieve its aim.

There are some structural arrangements which are clearly better than others, but there are no hard and fast rules which give the writer a precise blueprint for perfection. A great deal depends on the type of book that is being written. Not only can the subject be important, but also the book's style and purpose are influential.

The length of the book, its scope and its pace are linked to its framework. In building the skeleton of the book, you must know its approximate length and this will usually be agreed in the contract. The length will inevitably influence the book's scope. What must be included? What could be included? What can be left out? Will the subject be general or specific? Will some aspects be covered in depth? If so, which aspects and in which chapters? Some sections of the book may lend themselves to more superficial coverage; if so, which?

The final division of a book into its chapters requires careful thought. Each chapter should cover a specific major aspect of the book or, where appropriate, more than one aspect.

There is no precise formula one can use as a yardstick. The number of chapters is dictated by the nature of the book, its length and the natural divisions which seem appropriate. The ideal length of a chapter is, like the length of the book, that which it requires to put over its message.

You may find that certain chapters, which you thought were important, must be pruned to provide fuller coverage for the vital aspects of others. Some chapters may even be sacrificed. Care is very necessary here, for selection without considerable thought could ruin a good book.

For many subjects, the order of the chapters will dictate the pace of the book. Few books could sustain a full gallop from beginning to end and most writers agree that it would be undesirable to try to do so. A more leisurely chapter here and there allows the reader to 'draw breath' before being hustled along on the next episode of, for example, an account of high adventure.

Conversely, essential but boring chapters should be interspersed with more exciting material. For example, a chapter on the equipment which should be carried on a trip to the Amazon would only interest those readers intent on going and not the armchair reader.

In some cases, pace is irrelevant. This is particularly true of the text-book or any work which is concerned with the bald facts, probably set out in logical or chronological order. The reader requires the information, not the pleasure of reading a piece of beautiful literature. However, this does not mean that such books are not improved by good writing, with colourful descriptions and a convincing point here and there.

Chapter order

A straightforward school text-book would normally be expected to start at the educational grade for which it is intended and move progressively to the end.

A do-it-yourself book, although normally progressive, might

be structured in different ways. If the book is confined to one large project, it could start with the materials required and then move step-by-step through the various operations to completion. A book on a series of projects might begin with the easiest and work on through the increasing degrees of difficulty.

Although an autobiography often begins with the author's earliest memories and continues chronologically until the time of writing, it could use the technique, well-known to fiction writers, called 'flashback'.

This might paint in the picture of the author's present situation, his or her appointment as Prime Minister, perhaps, the book then returning to the author's youth to show how this success was achieved.

Start with the synopsis which was submitted to the publisher. In this you will have placed the chapters in some semblance of order, but it will only be a draft. It is possible that the publisher may have commented on any problems.

Using your synopsis, select those chapters which have obvious positions. Ask yourself if there are any chapters which lead into one another. Are there any chapters which can only be fully understood with the prior information from a preceding chapter? Are there any adjacent chapters which are essential, but are less interesting than the others? It might be desirable to avoid having such chapters next to each other in case they slowed the pace of the book too much. Instead, it might be possible to insert a stronger chapter between them.

For the shuffling around process, it is often helpful to write the chapter titles on separate sheets of paper. Add the salient points to be covered in each chapter, together with any comments on natural association or clashing between the chapters. As the sequence becomes more evident, the sheets can be given their provisional chapter numbers.

The first and final chapters usually have special roles to play. The first chapter opens the book and, in the absence of an introduction, it introduces the subject. The last chapter closes the book. These aspects will be fully covered later.

At this stage, it may be difficult to visualise the book as a balanced whole. Throughout the writing of the book, other factors inevitably emerge which can affect the structure. Chapter shifting can usually be done with little difficulty at any time. However, it is important to ensure that moving the order of chapters does not alter the logical sequence of information. In other words, the understanding of a chapter must not depend on information from a preceding chapter which has now been shifted to a later position in the book. This is an easy error to make and might slip by undetected until read by fresh eyes.

Filing research material

It is valuable to have a simple means of gathering your book material into rough chapters and filing it, together with the draft and progressively edited typescripts of the chapters. I use a foolscap manilla pouch. As it gets a great deal of handling, it is a good idea to get a strong one made of heavy material with linen reinforced gussets. In this I put foolscap cardboard file dividers, those with little tabs at the top. I label the tabs with the chapter numbers.

I use foolscap rather than A4 because it gives plenty of room to take the mass of material which builds up as the work proceeds.

The pouch comes into use as soon as I have decided on the chapter numbers. Into the chapter compartments goes anything I collect which is relevant to that chapter. These may be ideas which have come into my head, even in the middle of the night, and are jotted down on a piece of paper. A tear-sheet from a magazine article, a shrewd comment or criticism from one of my students, an answered questionnaire, something heard on the radio, a pamphlet, in fact anything which is relevant to the subject and might be useful, all are tucked away in the pouch.

When the time comes to write the chapter, these bits and pieces are taken out and read carefully. Some are discarded, some shifted to other chapters and those which remain are used to influence my thoughts on the draft of the chapter.

Getting the words right

The actual technique of selecting the right words, stringing them together and clearly expressing your thoughts is a tougher proposition. If you have already cut your teeth on writing magazine articles, then you probably have these skills already. If you can write a good letter or tell a good story, you are half-way there.

There is the mistaken idea that to be a successful writer requires a good education and being steeped in literature from a tender age. This is not so. The seeing eye, the selective mind and the power of self-expression are the real talents required.

Correct spelling is no insuperable obstacle when a good dictionary is only an arm's length away. Grammar can be polished with the right books or evening classes. Above all, plenty of sound reading of good books of your genre is the finest training.

Much of non-fiction is concerned with passing on information. To this end it must be factually accurate and clearly understandable. There is no room for woolly thinking or expression.

Generally, short sentences are better conveyors of information than long ones. Lengthy convoluted sentences are tedious and often obscure their intended message. They are the sentences which can only be understood if read more than once.

Too many short sentences together can give a staccato effect which may be irritating. However, used deliberately in appropriate places, they can give a punchy style which may be very effective.

Reading your writing aloud is an excellent way of checking its flow and balance. When you read it, it is essential to give the appropriate pause at punctuation – a brief pause at commas and a longer one at full-stops. Where there is no punctuation, read straight on. If you find yourself running out of breath, you will know that you are suffering from a serious shortage of punctuation as well. Reading aloud also shows up repetition of the same word or lack of euphony.

Relatively short paragraphs are preferable to very long ones. However, a number of two-line paragraphs appearing in the text together looks odd and usually reads poorly. The exception of course, is dialogue.

Some non-fiction books lend themselves to the inclusion of dialogue. If so, use it. It can bring an added vitality to otherwise dry passages.

Books on writing

There are many books on the art of writing. They range from the superficial to the almost indispensable. *The Way To Write* by J. Fairfax and J. Moat, published by Elm Tree, is a good primer. *Fowler's Modern English Usage*, Oxford University Press, is considered a sound guide to grammar. *The Nuts And Bolts Of Writing*, by Michael Legat, is an excellent book for beginners. It includes chapters which explain the basic rules of grammar and punctuation in a way which is very easily understood. I use two dictionaries, one paperback beside me and a large, heavy and comprehensive edition on the bookshelf for those knotty problems.

One of my students introduced me to *The Fontana Guide To Modern Thought* and I find it an excellent up-to-date reference book. It is said to 'take key terms from across the whole range of modern thought, set them within their context and offer short explanatory accounts (anything from ten to a thousand words) written by experts, but in simple language'. There are plenty of cross-references and reading lists.

Roget's Thesaurus is a book I feel I should need, but, in practice, I very rarely use it. Some writers regard it as an old reliable friend.

Readers' Digest's *The right word at the right time* is excellent and provides help with the use of difficult words and expressions.

There are a great number of other books which can be particularly helpful to those who stand at the cross-roads, pen in hand, wondering which way to go. There are books which, in one volume, cover every kind of writing from readers' letters to scripts for TV serials. Most of these books are not intended to give you more than a brief introduction to any one genre. They outline them all and then expect you, after you make your choice, to look for the specialised book, like this one, for example.

Non-linear thought patterns

One important piece of paper in each compartment of my manilla pouch is the non-linear thought pattern for that chapter. Readers of my book *The Way To Write Magazine Articles* will be familiar with this very useful way of marshalling thoughts and material. One pattern is normally used for each article but, for a book, a pattern can be used for each chapter. In fact, an initial pattern could even help to build the book framework.

Non-linear thought patterns, or flow of thought patterns as they are sometimes called, are no innovation for they have been around for a long time. There are several schools of thought, but they all follow a similar principle. One type of thought pattern is described in Tony Buzan's excellent book, *Use your head*, BBC Publications.

Briefly, our usual way of thinking and note-taking is linear. This is due to the way we are educated and the way we write and read. One thought follows another and we usually note them down successively, rather like a shopping-list. The problem is that each new note on a fresh line tends to preclude further thought and expansion of the preceding one.

In practice, our brain functions in a non-linear manner,

monitoring, processing and recording all manner of information at the same time.

Non-linear thought patterns avoid the constraints of linear patterns by having a central focus point from which the thoughts radiate out like the spokes of a wheel. Each spoke is free to divide and sub-divide as new thoughts stimulate avenues for fresh exploration.

An example of its use in chapter building will explain it more clearly.

Let us suppose that you are writing a book on gardening. You may decide to follow current trends and include a chapter on organic gardening, despite the fact that you may know little about it. Your first linear notes may be very basic and could look something like this:

ORGANIC GARDENING
What is it?
Any benefits?
Any disadvantages?
How is it done?
No chemicals.

If, however, you draw a non-linear pattern with 'organic gardening' at its hub and the other thoughts radiating out from it, it allows you freely to develop each thought.

Once your pattern is fully developed, you will have some idea of the amount and quality of its content. For example, you may find that the chapter would be weak in material and should either be a short one or, perhaps, linked with another related chapter.

Conversely, you may find that there is a wealth of material, all appropriate and worth using. So much, perhaps, that it will require more than one chapter or it might even be sufficient for a future book on the subject.

Presuming that the organic gardening pattern is to be used for one chapter only, how should it be used?

Because there is ample material there, it will probably be

impossible to cover each aspect in depth. To do so would give undue emphasis to the subject and might unbalance the book.

The method of drawing the patterns gives an immediate appreciation of the general association between the various points.

On examining the pattern, you will see that the salient points are nearer the centre and, as you move outwards, the finer points become evident. New points can easily be added as thought develops. Associated points can be linked, either by lines, by circling the points with the same coloured pen or by using coloured translucent highlight pens.

If an aspect of your pattern is a very important one, it might dominate the others and suggest that it should be developed separately with its own pattern. It often pays to do this, in order to develop that aspect fully. You may then find that it could even sustain a separate chapter.

The diagram gives a typical pattern for our organic gardening chapter, with one aspect highlighted for possible special development.

From selected areas of the pattern, I choose the chapter opening, the major points which must be put over and, perhaps, the point with which to end. Armed with this plan, I write my chapter, selecting the order of the main points and introducing the minor points as I go.

I then edit the chapter before putting it away in the manilla pouch and moving on to another chapter.

As I use a word-processor, I store two copies on disc and file the printed copy, known as a hard copy, in the pouch.

The gathering of material is an ongoing exercise and I shall expect to have more notes, tear-sheets, newspaper cuttings tucked into the pouch before I begin editing the book. If I feel this material is useful, it will be incorporated, even at a very late stage.

Even after the book is completed, the thought patterns should never be discarded. They are invaluable concise notes which can be used in future magazine articles or further books on the same subject.

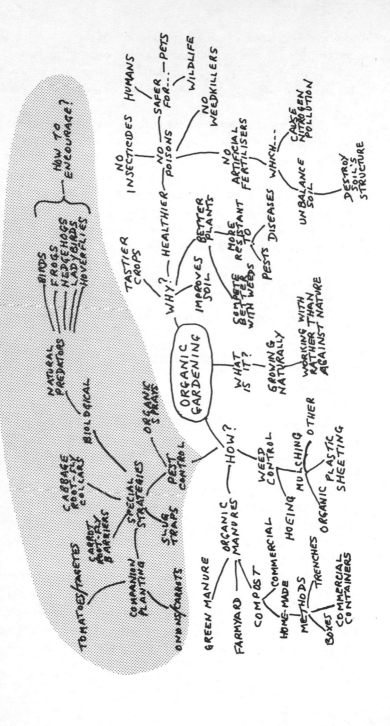

Writing the chapters

The chapters are the substance of the book. They are the flesh on the skeleton framework, permitting the author to use his own words and express the material in his own style. Given the same framework and the same material, any two writers would produce entirely different books. One might well succeed and the other might fail, everything depending on the author's unique viewpoint, his style and his power of expression.

Being faced with your first book can seem very daunting. Just getting started can be a tough obstacle. Most writers become experts in procrastination, convincing themselves that there are valid reasons why they should tackle that particularly difficult piece tomorrow, rather than today. Call it writer's block or just plain laziness, if you wish, but one thing is certain, you must overcome it.

With most fiction books, continuity is the essence of the story. Not only can 'grass-hopping' be irritating, but it is also very difficult to write effectively. With many non-fiction books, such strong continuity may not be so vital and is often replaced by a connecting thread which joins together the relatively self-contained chapters. Of course, there are many exceptions: biographies, travel, practical books, for example.

The advantage of the self-contained chapters for the writer is that the order in which chapters are actually written hardly matters.

Starting with the chapter which promises to be the easiest to write is a sound technique, particularly for new authors. When you have even one draft chapter filed away, it will bring a new confidence and you will be on your way. Remember the saying: 'Even a journey of a thousand miles begins with one step.'

For those who have trouble getting started from time to time, I recommend the book *Becoming a writer* by Dorothea Brande, published by Papermac. It is packed with wisdom and is still selling well, despite the fact that it was first published over fifty years ago.

Whether you use a typewriter or word-processor, before committing printed word to paper or keyed word to disc, you should be well-versed in the presentation of the professionally laid out typescript for a book. If you are at all uncertain of how to lay out a typescript so that it is understandable and acceptable to both publisher and printer, then you should read the chapter on 'The professional typescript' before proceeding.

It will save you a great deal of time, particularly if using a word-processor, if you lay out your work conventionally from the beginning, rather than revising it into the recognized style at a later stage.

Some writers polish each chapter to near perfection before moving on to the next. My own approach is to lick each chapter into no more than reasonable shape at this stage. It is, perhaps, a psychological quirk, but I prefer to get the main text of the whole book under my belt before I get down to the minutiae of the fine editing and polishing.

With the whole book in rough draft, I know how much time I have for the editing. I am aware from experience that I am unable to produce my best work under pressure. Seeing the date for completion looming ahead with two or three chapters yet to write is not the stimulus which suits me.

Everyone works differently. Some writers, painters, actors find that stress brings out the best in them. You will have to discover what turns your talent on and, of course, what turns it off.

The first and last chapters

In all but text-books, reference books and drier forms of non-fiction, the first chapter should have the power to capture the reader's interest. Indeed, even these exceptions could often benefit from more vitality in their first chapters.

Although some bookshop browsers choose their books by the authors' names, this is probably less true of non-fiction. Most people are attracted by the title and the cover. Then they may study the illustrations or read the 'blurb'. After that, they may read the opening of the first chapter.

If that first chapter fails to hold the reader's interest, he won't be with you for the second chapter. So you must read and re-read your first chapter, particularly its opening. Its factual content must be shuffled around until it satisfies you.

The opening of the first chapter must be positive in its initial presentation. It may stress the book's ability to fulfil the promise of its title, 'Become a wildlife photographer', 'Learn French in two months', 'Improve your golf'.

Take these two possible opening sentences for the beginning of this book – 'Even the name non-fiction describes what it is not, rather than what it is', or 'The field of non-fiction offers a wealth of opportunity for today's writers'.

Both are valid facts and could be used as possible book openings. The first is negative and would set a depressing tone to the beginning – a sort of 'Well, everything is against us, but we'll win through if we're lucky' attitude.

The second is positive and spells out confidence in the reader's chances of success. 'There is a wealth of opportunity.' The word 'wealth' was chosen rather than 'plenty' or other similar words. It is saying that there is great opportunity and implies that this book will tell you how to seize it. Later it washes in the negative facts along the lines of 'It is true that the name non-fiction doesn't help, but . . .'

The first chapter need not be long. The first paragraph can be short and to the point. The main essential is that it arrests the attention.

Take the all-time world best-seller, which happens to be non-fiction. The opening of the first chapter is simple. 'In the beginning God created the heaven and the earth.' Just try improving on that.

★

The final chapter rounds off the book, bringing it to a satisfying conclusion. It should do so competently. Some books just fizzle out, leaving the reader wondering if there are pages missing. Again, the way the final chapter performs its task depends very much on the type of book.

A text-book simply comes to the end of its intended scope, fourth year algebra or a history of the Tudor period, for example.

A travel book, covering a journey to the upper reaches of the Amazon might end on the safe return of the expedition or a look at the future of the region. It could have as its final chapter advice for those wishing to follow the same route, supplies to take, contacts for back-up services and sources of further information. These could, of course, be covered in appendices instead.

A practical book, this one for example, can give the reader a reassuring pat on the back before he puts the book's advice to the test.

Again, we are faced with the great multiplicity of non-fiction books. There is no clear format which can be applied to every type or even to the majority. The writer must work out for himself how his book should end and the final criterion must be his satisfaction with it.

Chapter Eight

The final stages

In the previous chapter I explained that my method of working is to leave each chapter in fairly rough draft until I can consider the book as a whole. Only then can I check that a chapter is fulfilling its intended function within the book and also in association with its adjacent chapters. After that I try to polish each chapter, and the book itself, to as near perfection as I can manage. I reason that there is little point in spending valuable time editing text which, after viewing the whole book, I may ultimately discard.

At this stage, you must read your book several times, noticing any places where the transition from one chapter to another lacks smoothness. If so, check to see if the ending of one chapter or the beginning of the next can be polished a little to improve matters.

If two chapters' association seems really discordant, perhaps the chapter order should be changed or material from one transferred to the other. If so, now is the time to try it out. Again, check to see that the chapter's new position fits comfortably with neighbouring chapters. Of course, the same need for harmony applies to a lesser degree to sections within a chapter or even adjacent paragraphs.

If you feel that a chapter is not strong enough to stand alone, perhaps it would be better incorporated into another chapter on an associated aspect.

Check your illustrations. Have you sufficient? If not, can you get more? Are your illustrations of high enough quality? Where will they appear in the text?

You must decide whether or not the book fulfils the promise of its title. Has any important point been left out? You may fully understand some of the book's more difficult aspects, but will everyone else? Is something more needed to facilitate the average reader's understanding? One way to check this is to get someone who is inexperienced in the subject to read the typescript and give an honest opinion.

Editing

At the editing stage, it is important to read the typescript as many times as possible. It is a mistake to attempt to check the spelling, sense and construction all at the same time. I find the best method is to take one chapter at a time. My first check is for the sense and general construction. Then I check for spelling and typographical errors. Finally, I read the chapter aloud. This time I listen to the flow of words and the euphony.

If I find that a passage might be misleading or difficult to understand, if a word is repeated too often or if two words which sound alike are too close together, I make a note. Then I go back and rewrite or find substitute words. Your *Roget's Thesaurus* could help here.

It can be very helpful to have fresh eyes reading your work. I am very fortunate that my wife, Molly, is also a writer. We read each other's work and offer constructive criticism. Unless we have a point which is proving difficult and which we need to discuss, we find it best not to read the other's work until it is near completion. If others read your work as often as you do, they become just as satiated with your words as you are. It is easy for a writer to make the error of repeating the same phrase, sentence or even paragraph in two separate chapters. When you read the book over and over again, you may accept this repetition in the mistaken belief that you last saw it in a previous reading of the book, not in another chapter. A completely fresh eye should spot this error immediately.

The publisher's editor will be reading the typescript with a critical eye, but, like all of us, will not be infallible. Despite repeated readings by author and editor, simple errors can slip by undetected, even appearing in the ultimate published work. It is up to you to ensure that your book is error free, firstly by submitting a typescript as near perfect as possible and, secondly, by very careful checking at the proof-reading stage.

Prelims and end-pages

You may already have decided – and discussed with your publisher – whether the book should have a foreword, introduction, index etc. Now, as the book nears its final draft, is a good time to write these in full. Those appearing in the front of the book are called 'prelims' or preliminary papers and those at the end are called end-pages. More details of these are given in the chapter on the professional typescript.

The inclusion of the various prelims and end-pages will probably have been agreed with the publisher. It is usual to have several of these pages, but it would be rare to include them all.

Foreword
The foreword or preface is often written by someone eminent in the subject of your book or, indeed, it could be written by any well-known personality. The idea is to increase the book's credibility and, if the writer of the foreword is sufficiently important, their name may even be printed larger on the cover than that of the author. The hope is that, by having this big name associated with the book, it will increase its saleability. Personally, I am not entirely convinced. However, if you have such a person up your sleeve, it would be wise to tell the publisher.

One thing which has concerned me is what you would do if the celebrity's foreword is unacceptable. For example, it might be in contradiction to some points in the book. Do you send it back and ask for it to be changed? Do you edit it and send it back for approval, plead shortage of space and ask them to agree to the amendments? If all else fails, you could say the publisher has decided against a foreword and drop it altogether. Much depends on how well you know the person and how conflicting the material is. It also depends on whether the approach to the celebrity was negotiated by you or the publisher. If the latter, then you can leave it to the publisher to sort out.

Introduction

The introduction is usually a page or two which, as the name implies, introduces the book. It may explain the book's purpose, how it should be used to best advantage, or even why it was written.

The introduction could, in some cases, fit better as a first chapter and vice-versa. There are no hard and fast rules here. In doubtful cases, it is up to the writer to use his discretion and then leave the final decision to the publisher.

The introduction usually follows the foreword in the order of the book.

List of contents

The list of contents will normally give chapter numbers, chapter titles and the page number on which the chapter commences. At this stage the page numbers will not be known and must be left until the page proofs arrive. It is useful to give the folio numbers, that is to say the typescript page numbers, as an interim guide.

List of illustrations

The illustrations are listed by title (or brief description) and by page number. Again, folio numbers can be inserted temporarily. If the captions on the illustrations are brief, then these could be given instead of the title.

Index

Your contract will state whether you will be responsible for any index. If you are, it will be up to you whether you do it yourself or get it done for you.

Most authors writing with a word-processor will have the facility to use a simple data-base to sort out words into alphabetical order. This can be done at the touch of a key, virtually instantaneously.

To compile the material for the index you must read your book, selecting every significant word which you feel should be in the index and also noting its folio appearance.

If you have no word-processor and data-base, you will be slower, but no less effective, using a manual sorting method.

The best way of indexing manually is to write, on a separate card, each word to be included in the index, noting the folio number at every occurrence and sorting the cards out into alphabetical order as you go. Then type out the list, with double-spacing between each item.

Complications occur when index sub-headings are required. As a simple example, if we consider a gardening book, we might have within the main index separate headings of 'flowers', 'vegetables', 'shrubs' etc. Under these headings, a sub-index of all the varieties of flowers, vegetables and shrubs would be given in alphabetical order.

A notorious error in indexing which must be avoided is constructing a 'maze'. The index may refer you to another heading, which in turn refers you back to the first heading. For example, again in your gardening book, you may find 'Cactus (see succulent)' and under succulent you may be referred back to cactus. In some cases, readers get a very complex run around before returning to the starting place. It is an easy mistake to make.

Also to be avoided is the long string of page references under the same subject, some references being to instances of mere passing mention. If faced with a tedious list of page references, readers often give up. If the page references seem too numerous, then you must be more selective. Scrap trivia and prune until only the more important references are retained. The introduction of more sub-headings may help.

The index is usually compiled from the page proofs. However, this means working under pressure of the deadline for return of the proofs. Despite the fact that it entails more work, it is well worth compiling the index from your typescript, using the folio numbers. This can be done after the typescript has been sent to the publisher. The folio numbers can be substituted by the page numbers on receipt of the page proofs.

For large non-fiction books, compiling an index can be time-consuming for the inexperienced. The author, eager to get on with other writing, may well decide to employ an indexer. As with the employment of any specialist, this can be expensive and can also introduce more delay at the proof stage. The publisher could organize this and charge the author, if appropriate.

Information on indexers available for such work can be obtained from the Registrar of The Society of Indexers or your publisher may recommend an indexer.

Bibliographies
Bibliographies can be useful to readers wishing to take the subject of your book further. It is important to check that facts are up-to-date.

Appendices
Appendices usually appear at the end of a book and may include tables, graphs, maps and other material which is more suitable for being presented collectively, rather than being scattered throughout the book.

Other miscellaneous inclusions
Certain other material may be included with the final typescript, such as acknowledgements, author's credits for other books, dedications etc.

Acknowledgements are a problem if you owe a great deal to

many people who assisted with the writing of the book. If you mention some, others who are left out may feel hurt. Sometimes it is better to generalise and express appreciation to all those whose contributions and advice made the book possible.

Your credits for the authorship of other books are usually best reserved for books on the same or similar subject. A book on do-it-yourself plumbing would gain little from the statement that you had also written a book on neurosurgical techniques. On the other hand, if your other books were of general interest, a reference to them might generate some new sales.

Dedications are a nice way of showing appreciation, perhaps to a member of the family or even to a group for their support or encouragement.

Illustrations

Your illustrations for the book will already have been earmarked. They may be in the form of photographs, drawings or even rough sketches which the publisher will have agreed to bring up to reproduction standards. There may also be tables, graphs and maps which may be distributed throughout the book or gathered together.

Further details of the layout of the book, together with its prelims and end-pages, are given in the following chapter on the professional typescript.

Chapter Nine

The professional typescript

Although all writers should try to be professional in every aspect of their work, much of this professionalism comes only with experience. Their typescript, however, is one area where writers can present a professional face from the earliest stages of their career and it certainly pays to do so.

Rest assured that the days when best-sellers could be written in pencil in school exercise books are over. When submitting a typescript, particularly a first one, you need every artifice working in your favour and that includes a clean, tidy, easily-read typescript.

All that is required is information on the conventional layout, together with the right tools and a little care and patience.

I know writers who cheerfully admit to being careless about their typescripts. As one writer told me: 'I am no typist and my typescript is always covered in alterations. If I have a contract and an advance on royalties, no publisher is going to back out just because the typescript isn't perfect.'

She was right, of course. No publisher looks for perfection, but there are other considerations which should encourage us always to submit the neatest typescript we can.

It is not unknown for a publisher to have a particularly untidy typescript re-typed and to charge the author for the cost. A really poor typescript can cause a great deal of extra work and the memory of it might linger a long time with the publisher. It could be an influence when your next book is being considered.

An untidy and much-altered typescript can cause mis-understandings of the text and also introduce typographical errors. If the typescript is a mess, it will be easier for errors to be overlooked both by yourself and by the publisher.

I know some writers never bother and just leave the publisher to sort it all out. However, if there is a right and a wrong way, why not form the habit of getting it right? If you ever consider self-publishing, you will have to do it the right way.

Finally, there is the natural pride in one's work. There is a great satisfaction in sending off a clean and tidy typescript, clearly the work of a craftsman and not an amateurish dabbler. If a writer likes to think of himself as a professional, then he should act like one. In the case of the typescript there is no practical reason for not doing so.

Advice from publishers

All publishers will give advice to their authors if asked for it. It is in their interests to do so.

Some publishers are very specific in their needs. David & Charles, for example, have an excellent booklet which they give to their authors. It ensures reasonable uniformity and must save both writers and publishers a great deal of time.

Others may not be so helpful. One first-time author told me that he had no advice from his publisher, but he sensibly sent off his first chapter for their approval of his layout. Back came the typescript with the terse comment: 'Double-spacing, please.'

He asked my advice, which I gave him. To his delight, his next submission brought a letter from the publisher congratulating him on his professional typescript.

The layout of the typescript should be conventional. This should always be adhered to, but is particularly important if the author is publishing the book himself. In the case of self-publishing, the typescript goes straight to the printer and he prints what you give him. There is no publisher's editor in between as a safeguard against errors.

There are many ideas on the best layout of typescripts and they vary widely. Fortunately there is a British Standard and, if we adhere to that, there can be few quibbles. The standard is BS5261, Part I, 1975, *Recommendations for preparation of typescript for printing*. Copies can be obtained from BSI, 2 Park St, London, W1A 2BS. It is quite expensive and, for all normal purposes, the information given in this chapter will suffice.

I have not tried to cover all the points in the British Standard, for that would be unnecessary and tedious. However, I have made every effort to cover all essentials.

You should use white A4 paper of reasonably heavy quality – about 70–80gms is ideal. American A4, which is a little wider and shorter than standard A4, is quite acceptable and is widely used in word-processor printers.

A black ribbon is essential. Never use coloured ribbons and guard against the gradual fading which often passes unnoticed. Change the ribbon as soon as it ceases to be dead black.

The typeface should be standard, pica or elite. Never use italic or script faces. The typeface must be clean and undamaged. Dirty typefaces tend to print solid blobs in closed letters and chipped faces can be unclear or even misleading. Both of these factors can cause mistakes in reading, editing and typesetting.

Manual and electric typewriters are rapidly falling from favour with writers and are being replaced by the highly effective word-processor. Such has been its impact on writers' efficiency and output that a separate chapter has been devoted to the subject.

The use of correction fluids is quite acceptable, providing the end result is neat and perfectly legible. I find correction papers to be less durable and not to be recommended.

There is no doubt that the word-processor really comes into its own in editing and correcting typescripts. It is a great boon, particularly for those who are not really competent typists.

Although corrections with a word-processor are simplicity itself, there are still occasions when an alteration in manuscript may be appropriate. For example, if a minor error is found in the final typescript, it is easier either to cross out neatly and insert the correction or to use correcting fluid, rather than to reprint the whole page. The best fluid I have found to date is in the Pentel Correction Pen.

Manuscript corrections should be kept within reasonable bounds and, if there are too many of them, you should retype. The criterion must be to achieve a neat and legible typescript which is quite unambiguous.

The layout

You should use only one side of the paper. Generous margins should be allowed all round, namely 40mms for the left margin and 25mms each for the right margin and the top and bottom of the page. Double-spacing must be used throughout.

The wide margins and double-spacing are essential for the publisher's editor to alter, correct, comment and provide instructions for the printer.

No extra space is needed between paragraphs. The commencement of another paragraph is indicated by indenting three spaces. The paragraphs commencing a chapter or following a sub-heading do not require indentation as their paragraph status is self-evident.

Punctuation

Punctuation, such as commas and full-stops, should be followed by one space only. Occasionally, writers become particularly attracted to some forms of punctuation and use them far too liberally and often incorrectly. Exclamation marks are only for exclamations and not for emphasis. Parentheses should be used sparingly, as should colons and semi-colons.

Underlining must only be used where the text is to be printed in italics, for that is what it indicates to the printer. Again, italicising should not be overdone.

Dialogue should be within single quotation marks. For quotes within quotes, double quotation marks are used. For example: 'She came up to me and cried, "Who are you?"'

Prelims

Many authors never bother with the detailed layout of dedications, acknowledgements, prefaces and other pages in the front of the book. They merely tell the publisher what they would like and then hope for the best. Again, with the growth in self-publishing, more authors are being forced to become conversant with formal layout.

The prelims are not numbered, but are given alphabetical letters commencing with A. The number of prelims used varies with each book, but will normally include some of the following: the half-title, the title page, the biblio page, dedication, foreword, preface, acknowledgements, list of contents, list of illustrations, introduction.

The half-title has only the title of the book. The title page will have the title, sub-title if any, author's name and the publisher's name.

The biblio page is completed by the publisher and includes the copyright, the publisher's and printer's names and addresses, the International Standard Book Number (ISBN) and other possible items.

The dedication is the author's prerogative to pay tribute to a person, persons or cause etc. The foreword is usually a comment on the book or its author by another person. The preface is comment by the author. If the preface is more than a page or so, it would normally be considered an introduction. Acknowledgements can be given a prelim of their own or incorporated in the preface or introduction.

The contents can be a simple list of chapter numbers, titles and page numbers, although at the typescript stage we would only know the folio numbers. Some books lend themselves to extended contents in lieu of an index. In this case, the chapter title is followed by a list of the sub-headings to be found in each chapter or a brief summary of the chapter's contents.

The list of illustrations can be similar to the list of contents, but probably including abbreviated versions of the captions.

The introduction may come before or after the contents and illustration lists. Much depends on the publishing house style. You can always look at a similar book by the same publisher, particularly if your book is one of a series.

If you require acknowledgements, dedications etc., then you must ensure the prelims for them are completed. If you get things in the wrong order, the publisher will sort them out, but with self-publishing, the onus is on you.

Using a separate sheet for each prelim, you put a letter of the alphabet in the top right hand corner and encircle it with a solid line to indicate that the letter is not to appear in the finished book. Unless instructed to the contrary, the printer will not set into type anything surrounded by such a line. The last prelim should be endorsed 'Last folio of the prelims'.

Although not essential, it can be helpful to include an inventory of the whole package of typescript and illustrations which is being sent to the publisher. This is a check list for the publisher and printer. It would look something like this:

Author's name and address.
Book title.
Date.
Inventory of complete typescript and illustrations.
Prelims (folios A–F)
Chapters 1–10 (folios 1–160)
Copy for illustrations Figs 1–6 (folios 161–166)
Plates 1–10.

This would be surrounded with a solid line, as already explained, and would be the first prelim. In fact, most authors appear to omit this inventory, but I believe it to be a sound practice.

The numbering of the text folios starts at 1 and continues in sequence to the end. The recognised position for numbering is the top right of each folio and the number is then circled with a pen. I have a draughtsman's template to help me draw a neat circle.

The title of the book is shown at the bottom left hand of each folio. This is important in case folios get mislaid in an office where there could be a large number of typescripts around.

Each chapter starts on a fresh folio with the chapter title. In the left hand margin opposite the title, you should write 'Chap', again enclosed in a solid line.

Sub-headings are also given a marginal indication, usually a letter 'A'. It is standard practice to draw a neat square round this letter. If a book has major and minor sub-headings, the former will usually have A in the margin and the latter B. Sub-headings are usually justified on the left and given their own line. These are called side-heads and are the type of sub-heading most commonly used.

If the sub-heading is centred on the line, it is usually printed in bolder or larger type. These are called cross-heads. It is wise to use side-heads in your typescript and to leave the publisher to make any variations.

Chapter headings are followed by an extra line-space. Sub-headings are preceded and followed by an extra line-space. Examples of chapter and sub-heading marginal indications are shown in the diagram.

End-pages

The end-pages consist of those folios which come after the main text. They may include a glossary, bibliography, appendices, index. They are given folio numbers as if they were part of the main text.

In articles, it is customary to type 'mf' at the bottom of each page, apart from the last, to indicate to the editor that there are

Chap — 2   The article market today

First of all, let us take a brief look at the market place for
articles.

Have you noticed how the magazine shelves of the big chain
bookshops have gradually extended in recent years? New magazines are
being launched all the time. It is true that some of them fail after
a couple of issues, but the overall trend is still upward. According
to the current <u>Willing's Press Guide</u> there are now over 11,000
magazines and newspapers in circulation in this country. This is
obviously to our benefit, for most of these magazines have some
potential for the reasonably competent freelance.

A — Factual articles and 'think-pieces'

The dictionary says that an article is 'a literary composition
dealing with a particular subject, forming part of a newspaper or
magazine.'

Writers see articles in a rather different light. True, there are
'literary' articles, those rather erudite pieces, but writers tend
to talk about 'factual articles,' 'think-pieces,' 'shorts,'
'short-shorts' and 'fillers'.

Factual articles are, as one would suppose, based on facts. The
facts can come from research or experience - 'Building a rockery
from scratch,' 'Restoring our canals,' 'The tragedy of Culloden
Moor,' for example.

Think-pieces range from home-spun philosophy to outbursts on a
favourite hobby-horse - 'Is marriage dead?' 'Why not restore
capital punishment?' 'Schoolgirl mothers.' Think-pieces often pose
questions which the writer then goes on to answer. Unfortunately,

Magazine articles

more pages to come. This avoids a lost page going unnoticed. This is unnecessary in non-fiction books if you include an inventory, but can be a useful alternative.

Illustrations

Drawings, sketches, graphs and tables are called figures and photographs are called plates. Marginal notes should be used to give the printer a clear indication of the position in which you would like the illustration to appear in the text.

All illustrations must be numbered. Photographic prints should be numbered on the back using a felt-tip pen, not a ballpoint. If prints are on resin-coated paper, then a spirit-based pen must be used. Captions for illustrations fulfil an important role. They must be clearly worded and concise. Type the numbered captions on a separate sheet of paper. Give the caption sheet a clear heading and folio number and include it in the end-pages.

Transparencies should have an adhesive paper peel-off dot on the mount. Write the number of the transparency on the dot. Type the captions on a separate sheet of paper, giving the dot number. This caption sheet should also be clearly headed, given a folio number and included in the end-pages.

Although there are individual preferences, most publishers dislike pins, staples and tags. Paper-clips are unpopular with some and a well-packed MS with no fastenings is quite acceptable and even preferred.

Illustrations are best placed in a manilla envelope and clearly labelled on the outside. I use a 'Photographs, please do not bend' sticker on the envelope, in case of mishandling in the publisher's office.

Finally, pack two copies of the complete typescript for dispatch. A good carbon copy is satisfactory for the second copy. Photocopies are also satisfactory, but are expensive. With a word-processor, you just run off two copies.

A strong cardboard box, such as is used for typing paper,

serves very well if the typescript is not too large. If necessary, stiffen with corrugated cardboard. Enclose the illustrations. Post it by registered post, particularly if there are valuable original transparencies enclosed.

Chapter Ten

The word-processor

A high proportion of writers make no claim to be typists. Some do go to the trouble of learning to touch-type and say that it is well worth it. Others persevere with two fingers and can achieve quite high speeds. Most of us, however, have begrudged spending time on learning to touch-type and have struggled on to the best of our ability.

For me, typing has always been a tedious business and the very worst aspect of writing. Using a typewriter to edit a book is sheer drudgery, even for the expert touch-typist. Correcting typographical errors, spelling mistakes and poor grammar can be bad enough, but re-writing whole passages, shifting text from one page to another, even re-writing entire chapters can be enough to put some would-be writers off the idea altogether.

For those of us who had been Cinderellas, chained to our typewriters for weeks on end, the word-processor came along and whisked us off to the ball. In my opinion, the word-processor is the best thing to happen to writers since the Chinese invented paper 2,000 years ago.

With a word-processor, editing a book is child's play. Blocks of text can be shifted about and juggled with at will. Masses of corrections on the same page no longer mean re-typing everything, for, at the touch of a key, it is re-typed for you at breakneck speed and with perfect copy.

In many cases, the words are counted for you, with even a spelling checker and perhaps a thesaurus thrown in.

A word-processor earns money by speeding up the mechanical processes of production, leaving the writer more time for that which he loves best, the creativity of writing.

Briefly, a word-processor consists of a keyboard, like that of a conventional typewriter, a visual display unit (VDU), similar to a TV screen, and a means of storing the output, either on floppy discs, which are removable for filing, or on a hard disc, which is retained within the machine. It is also necessary to have a printer which produces the typed material which is known as a hard copy.

There are dedicated word-processors, which perform no other function but word-processing, and there are word-processors based on micro-computers, which will perform a host of functions, even playing games and music. Most writers would be well advised to avoid the dedicated word-processors on the grounds of their limited function.

Your basic micro-computer may consist of only a keyboard within the case of which is the electronic memory, called Random Access Memory or RAM, which temporarily stores the material you are processing.

Unless you have a hard disc, you will require a disc-drive, to take the floppy discs which permanently store your work on file. You will need a VDU for viewing your work as you type it. Some manufacturers, Amstrad, for example, integrate the keyboard, disc-drive and VDU into the same package and, although they are separate pieces of equipment, they only function as a unit.

Choosing a micro

Choosing the right micro is a matter of equating the cash available with the purposes for which it is required, together with your personal taste.

Currently, the most common micros used by writers are the Amstrad machines. They are cheap, compact and efficient. Some, like the PC1512 and its clones, are IBM compatible and will take many of the programs designed for the IBM business machines.

Up-market machines for writers include the Apple Mackintosh which, although very powerful and with high quality programs, is considered by many to be over-priced.

In trying to find a micro, you should talk to a few writers who use them. You may find their varying opinions confusing, but speaking to only one writer can give you a distorted impression. I know some writers who are working perfectly happily with obsolete systems the names of which have been almost forgotten. They swear by them, but new machines will be far more efficient.

The Society of Authors will always give members an objective opinion on a word-processor, within the scope of the Society's reports from other members.

When buying your word-processor, you should go to a specialist computer dealer, not a shop which sells cameras, radios and TVs as well as computers. The specialist dealer is far more likely to be able to help you with your choice and give you back-up help if there are any teething troubles.

In addition, such a dealer will usually let you have 'hands-on' experience of the model of your choice and will not be too disturbed if you spend a few hours playing with it and studying the manual.

Printers

The printer is normally a separate purchase, although there are some package deals which include it. Printers range from the cheap and basic dot-matrix printer to the expensive and super quality laser printer.

Dot-matrix printers create the letters by printing a series of very fine dots which give the appearance of lines in the form of the letter. Those printers with sparse dots can print vertical and horizontal lines of quite good quality, E, H, for example, but diagonals and curves, such as S, N, are inferior in reproduction.

The more expensive models of dot-matrix printers produce better quality printing and are also much faster, often printing several hundred characters a second.

Even the cheaper dot-matrix printers may have the facility for switching from draft quality printing, which is fast, but lower grade, to a fine density print mode, which is slower, but gives a much more acceptable quality.

There are also daisy-wheel printers, which produce printing exactly like that of a typewriter. They are generally more expensive than dot-matrix printers and much slower. They are also less flexible in the variety of type-faces which are readily available.

Paper

Ideally, printers should be able to handle both single sheets and fan-fold paper. With fan-fold, the paper is in one continuous length, folded like a fan. The individual sheets have a fine perforated line between them which enables the sheets to be neatly separated. There are also perforated edging strips which have punched holes in them to take the teeth of the tractor-drive of the printer. This advances the paper with precision in rather the same way as a film is advanced in a camera. These strips also can be torn off neatly after printing.

The advantages of fan-fold paper are simplicity, precise alignment and the facility of printing large files without attention from the operator. This leaves the writer free to get on with other tasks.

Letters can be readily printed on fan-fold paper. With the great choice of type-faces on dot-matrix printers, it is easy to design an attractive letter-heading which is quite suitable for all but the most prestigious correspondence. This can be printed at will by the touch of a key.

Visual Display Units

Your choice of VDU depends largely on your personal taste. Those giving white characters on a black screen are perfectly acceptable, but many screens have green or orange characters on black or coloured background. People often favour a combination which they feel is more restful to their eyes. The problem is that you have no way of knowing what suits you until you have used it for some time.

Resist all temptations to buy an attractive-looking full-colour VDU, for it is expensive and usually has a much poorer resolution with less distinct characters. It is only needed if you have other uses for your micro, such as game playing.

Disc-drives

The disc-drive is essential for keeping your work on permanent file. This means that you can retrieve a file, add to it, delete parts of it and edit it in any way before saving it again on the disc for further editing or printing. The current work must be stored in this way or it would be lost when the micro is switched off.

Most word-processors offer the choice of floppy discs or hard discs. The floppy discs are rather like small record discs which are inserted into slots in the disc-drive. Each disc can store a considerable amount of material in its memory.

There is usually a further choice of single or twin disc-drives. You can manage with a single disc-drive, but it is slower and the constant swopping of discs which it entails can become tedious. The dual disc-drive is usually considered to be worth the extra cost.

A hard disc is permanently integrated in the micro. It has a large memory capacity. It is very fast in operation and speeds up most programs. It is also more expensive. I believe it is worthwhile, if you can afford it.

Word-processing programs

The most difficult item to select is the word-processing program which will actually drive your machine and turn it into a word-processor. There is an immense range, from inexpensive and simple programs with limited functions to those costing £500 or more. The latter give a great number of sophisticated functions, many of which would be superfluous for most writers.

The first function you will require is the ability to type your text and to see it on the screen, more or less as it will be typed by the printer. In jargon, this is known as WYSIWYG – 'What you see is what you get', although, as I have implied, this normally should be 'What you see is *more or less* what you get'.

You should be able to set up the required page format with the minimum of trouble, with margins, headers, footers, line spacing and tabulation.

Many writers insist on having a page-numbering facility, but, in practice, this is unnecessary. I find that, for books, numbering the folios in manuscript is the simplest method and can be done at the same time as other manuscript notations.

It should be possible to edit the text with the option of inserting words or overwriting existing text. As the words are inserted the paragraph should automatically reform itself within the set margins. Not all programs do this and having to reform manually by pressing designated keys after each insertion can be very irritating. So always check that 'auto-reform' is provided as a facility.

You should be able to mark blocks of text and delete them, copy them or move them around with ease. The latter enables you to juggle with the order of passages at will.

A 'search and replace' facility can be a great boon. If, for example, you had written a book on a small developing country which suddenly changed its name, the facility could be used with great effect. You would invoke the facility, type the old name, type the new name and press a key. Almost instantaneously, the name would be changed throughout the file.

A word-count facility is very useful, although many writers are quite happy without it. Some word counts have to be invoked, but others give a running count which is displayed on the screen throughout, giving you an instant tally. It is particularly important for article writers who are often working to precise length requirements.

The spelling checker could be valuable for those who are weak in this area. The document is searched for any word which fails to match up with the program's word list. If it finds one, it stops and offers suggestions of what the word might be. Some of these suggestions can be quite bizarre.

Some spelling checkers are extremely slow. If the number of words in the checker is fairly limited, it will be puzzled over any word which is slightly out of the ordinary, considering it a spelling error and slowing the check down still further.

Some of us have the typing weakness of transposing a couple of letters, spelling 'and' as 'adn', for example. The spelling checker will spot these for you. However, careful editing should pinpoint them anyway.

The more comprehensive word-processing programs take up a lot of the computer's memory. If your micro has a modest memory, the program could occupy most of it, leaving insufficient for a reasonably long text for you to work on. For this reason, it is essential to find out not only whether your proposed choice of micro and word-processing program will be compatible, but if it will also leave you ample memory for a document of good length.

In searching for your word-processor, it can be useful to have a browse through a few copies of the appropriate computer magazines. For example, one of the magazines which specialise in micros could help you with your choice of micro, after which you could look at one of the several magazines which deal specifically with the micro of your choice and its associated programs.

When you have made your choice, you may wish to look at the magazines which specialise in advertisements for equipment at cut-prices. You will find the lowest market prices, but mail order purchases are not always the best buys for newcomers to this field. The support of a friendly local dealer can help you through the common beginners' problems and may be well worth the extra you will have to pay.

Micro-computers and word-processing programs are advancing in technology and reducing in price at such a rate that it is impractical to recommend specific models and programs. Those in popular use today will probably be superseded by the time this book is published. It will be up to you to satisfy yourself that you are getting the best value for your money and the package which will most suit your needs.

An increasing number of publishers are accepting the text of books on floppy discs from authors. They also require a 'hard copy', i.e. a printed copy. This has become more common with the arrival of inexpensive micro-computers which are compatible with commercial computers.

The great benefit for the publisher is that, by the addition of coding, your disc can be used by the printer without the cost of ordinary typesetting. Much depends on the compatibility of your system with that of the printer, although conversions from some systems to others are possible.

The question of submitting text on disc should be cleared with the publisher at the time of signing the contract. If you are well enough acquainted with word-processing to insert the coding yourself, then you should be able to negotiate better terms in your contract as it is a great saving to the publisher.

If you are considering self-publishing, then using coded text on disc is a far more interesting proposition and should be gone into carefully. A useful book, but with an awesome title, is *A guide to authors' symbolic pre-press interfacing codes* from British Printing Industry Federation, 11, Bedford Row, London, WC1R 4DX.

Finally, I truly believe that a word-processor is so valuable that every writer should consider buying one. It could be a worthwhile investment of that advance on royalties from your book.

Chapter Eleven

Before publication

After the typescript has been dispatched to the publishers, the author usually has a respite. The publisher may be in touch with queries, suggestions for amendments or minor changes. Sometimes, the publisher will require major alterations, particularly if it is suspected that the book may attract legal action as it stands.

If radical changes are proposed, it is often a good idea to make an appointment to call on the publisher to discuss matters. Listen carefully to any proposals and the reasoning behind them. Be prepared to argue your case if you disagree. However, your contract will require you to make any alterations which are deemed necessary and, if you fail to do so, your contract could be terminated and you would probably be required to repay your advance.

You must remember that the publisher is in business to sell books and this includes your book. He is unlikely to create unnecessary problems on a mere whim. At the end of the day, you would be wise to bow to his greater experience and fall in with his wishes, unless it would be contrary to your principles.

Blurbs and other publicity

Publishers vary in their attitudes to authors' involvement in cover design and the wording of the blurb, etc. If you have good ideas, don't hesitate to air them, but be prepared to have them rejected. Some books, like this one, for example, are part of a series and the cover follows a similar pattern throughout the series. The publisher will wish to adhere to this, particularly if the series is proving successful.

If you are invited to write the blurb, you should consider doing so. If you are unhappy about writing your own blurb, the publisher will do it for you and submit a draft for your approval.

It is an important part of the book and people do read it. They want to know, briefly, what the book is about. They also read it to find out about the author – who he is and why he is qualified to write such a book.

Check how many words the publisher requires and ask for guidance on the kind of blurb preferred. Then jot down the main points you wish to make. Don't be too modest, for shyness sells few books. Be honest, but selective. Don't try to tell your life's history.

Depending on the type of book, some publishers like you to give a few homely details. For example, one of our blurbs included the fact that my wife and I live in an old rural cottage with a half-wild cat and a bevy of half-tame bats. Sometimes they like you to state your partner's profession and even how many children you have. All these points should be cleared with the publisher in advance or, with a series, you could study some of the earlier books.

Choose your words carefully. Bring out all the positive sales points. Think of the factors which would influence you if you were considering buying the book. Edit it and polish it until it is the best piece of succinct promotion of which you are capable, but within the bounds of the truth.

Some publishers like a photograph of the author with the blurb. These are known as 'mug shots'. It is wise to have a few of these in varied attire and poses to match the subject of your writing. Keep a few prints of these in hand as they are useful for other publicity purposes, as well as for books and articles.

Page proofs

The arrival of the proofs heralds the next major job for the author. Most publishers these days seem to go straight into page proofs which, as the name implies, come in page form just as they will appear in the book. Apart from illustrated books, galley proofs, in which the printed text arrives on long lengths of paper, are rarely seen by authors, unless they are involved in self-publishing.

You will be expected to examine the proofs minutely for errors. You will make appropriate corrections on the proofs and return them promptly. The time allowed will be stated in your contract, and confirmed when the proofs are sent to you: it is usually between two and three weeks.

The purpose of the proofs is to permit meticulous corrections of genuine errors, not for authors to have second thoughts about a better turn of phrase or making a new point.

If you edited your final script carefully, the number of errors attributable to you should be minimal. Your contract will state that the cost of correcting any authors' errors above, say, 10% of the total typesetting cost, will be yours. That may sound generous, but the cost of correction is very expensive and is out of all proportion to the original cost of typesetting. Very few errors will absorb the 10% and could leave you with a big bill to pay. The answer is, of course, to ensure your final typescript is as near perfect as possible.

In the unfortunate case of a major error having been made by you in the original typescript, it must be corrected no matter what the cost. Sometimes errors may emerge which are no fault of the author. For example, facts which were correct at the time of writing may have become outdated or overtaken by events. In all cases of major error, liaison with the publisher is necessary on how best to solve matters with the minimum of trouble and, of course, expense.

When making alterations you should try to contain the wording within the space occupied by the original. In other words, it is important to avoid the addition of a few words shunting the printing on for page after page until you reach a blank space which can contain it, possibly at the end of a chapter. It can often be done effectively by a little re-phrasing and re-arranging of adjacent passages.

It must be remembered that all extensive alterations run the risk of introducing further errors, more expense and further delay, causing frustration to publisher and author alike.

Proof-correcting methods

The method of correcting proofs must follow conventional lines in order that the publisher and printer can fully understand the significance of the author's marks. There is a British Standard which lays down the recommendations for proof correction. It is BS5261, Part 2, 1976. It gives the full details necessary for all contingencies in proof correction. In practice, a far more useful précis of the British Standard is given in *The Writers' and Artists' Year Book* published by A & C Black.

It is customary to correct all typographical errors (i.e. mistakes made by the typesetters in setting the book) in red ink and all others in black or blue. The indications of the errors and their corrections are made in the text and/or in the margins. Those in the text indicate the location and the nature of the error, the marginal notes being complementary and explanatory. If several errors occur on the same line, both margins can be used to avoid confusion.

The symbols and indications used are fairly simple and more or less logical. It is important that you should use the conventional symbols rather than trying to explain your wishes in words or, worse still, using symbols which mean something to you and probably nothing to the publisher and printer.

Check and double-check the proofs. This will be your last chance to make essential corrections. The publisher's editor will also be checking a copy, but, although typographical errors may seem fairly obvious, errors in the actual text may only be recognised by the author. Although one could reasonably expect that no typographical errors would escape two pairs of eyes, all too often they seem to slip through unnoticed.

You must return the proofs to meet your contracted deadline. Publishers work to tight schedules and plan in anticipation of the author's reasonable co-operation.

With the proof completed and returned, there will be further breathing space of several months before publication. This is a good time to be thinking of your next book. In practice, it is likely that the ideas will have been germinating in the back of your mind for some time. Now start cultivating them.

If you are an article-writer, you should consider contacting some of your regular editors to re-establish yourself and offer them some work. Editors have notoriously short memories and there are plenty of writers waiting to fill the slot you left empty. In particular you should keep in touch with the editors of those magazines which could prove useful in promoting your book. This aspect will be developed later.

Chapter Twelve

The business side

Some writers bury themselves in their writing and try to ignore the business side. They may mislay material, lose correspondence, fail to meet deadlines and, if their writing becomes profitable, they can fall foul of the tax man. Although many writers find the business side tedious, sooner or later they recognise that careful attention to it is very necessary.

Records

If you are a published writer, then you are in business with all that it entails. You are, at least to some degree, self-employed. You will receive royalties and you will incur expenses. Even if you are uninterested in your profitability, the details must be recorded in order to arrive at your tax liability, if any. You have a statutory responsibility to declare your earnings for tax purposes and this cannot be avoided. In addition, as a self-employed person you might even have a responsibility for meeting the payments for insurance stamps.

The business side includes having suitable filing systems for research material, correspondence, finances, photographic and other illustrations. It is essential that the system allows work to be retrieved easily when required.

The details of your painstaking research are valuable, for they probably had a great deal of time and money invested in them.

The material can be used for magazine articles and, possibly, future books. If it is stored in a haphazard fashion, at the very best it will take time to find and time is precious to the busy writer.

The actual material will usually be in the shape of notes, tear-sheets, newspaper cuttings, photocopies and other bits and pieces. An easy way of storing these is to gather them into manageable sized sub-divisions and put each sub-division into a manilla envelope, suitably labelled. These envelopes can then be placed in box-files and stored upright on book shelves. Major subjects may either occupy more than one box-file or, more economically, can be stored in heavy-weight A4 manilla wallets. These may be stored on edge in the same way as the box-files.

Index systems

A few writers use their micro-computers for filing all their research material, but many had so much material before the coming of the computer that it would be too time-consuming to transfer it. Most authors seem to be content with manual systems and some, like my wife and me, use both.

A card index system is preferred by most authors. It is straightforward and, if properly organised and kept up to date, can be very effective. It scores particularly on cheapness and simplicity.

You can usually get a local printer to sell you surplus card, white or pastel-coloured. Get him to guillotine it to an appropriate size. We use 125 x 100mms. It pays to have a few cut to 125 x 125mms, which can be trimmed to leave 25mm tabs to use as markers for separating sections. The title of the section can be written on the tab. Stagger the position of the tabs so that they are not covering each other.

These cards can be stored on edge in any convenient box. Steel cabinets, custom-built for the job, are ideal, but they are expensive if bought new. In practice, any suitably sized box will suffice.

Try to keep the system fairly simple. The Dewey Decimal System is excellent for public libraries, but would be needlessly complex and unwieldy for the average writer. Most writers focus their attention on a relatively narrow range of subjects and, for them, a simple alphabetical index is probably the best way.

Major subjects will probably have a great deal of material and it usually pays to use a sub-index in the file, each with a sub-index card under the main heading.

The appropriate index card should lead you straight to the material in question. Clearly there must be a reference to the box-file or wallet and then to the specific manilla envelope containing the material.

It sounds complex, but in practice it works well. The essential factor is keeping it up-to-date and returning material to the right place when you have finished with it.

Filing illustrations

Illustrations will come in a variety of forms. There will probably be negatives, 254 x 203mm prints, contact sheets, transparencies, photocopies and, possibly, tear-sheets.

Illustrations are valuable and originals are very precious, many of them probably being irreplaceable. It pays to take the greatest care of them.

Negatives are best stored in ring-backed binders, specially designed for the purpose. These binders hold a supply of plastic divided wallets. The 35mm films are cut into strips of six exposures and each strip given its own compartment in the plastic wallet, with seven strips to each wallet. The 120-size films are cut into strips of three exposures and are filed four strips to a wallet.

My binders are labelled A1, A2 etc. for 35mm film and B1, B2 etc. for 120 film. Each wallet is identified numerically and each strip is lettered A–G. Each negative is further numbered from left to right. Each binder has its loose-leaf index in the front and every negative appears in the main index under its subject. A negative in folder A5, wallet 14, strip E, negative 2 would have the reference A5/14E2.

Black and white enlargements which are either surplus or have been returned by publishers after use are filed under their negative references. These references are written carefully on the back of these prints before submission. Contact sheets are filed with their negatives.

I find the easiest way to store 35mm transparencies is in straight plastic magazines for projectors. These carry 50 slides. Two magazines, totalling 100 slides, fit into a neat plastic box. The boxes stack easily and they are surprisingly cheap.

As 120-size transparencies are unmounted, they are flimsy and vulnerable. These come back from most processing laboratories in plastic sleeves in wallets of twelve. It is convenient to keep them in these, suitably indexed.

Correspondence

Again, simplicity is all important. Box-files can be purchased with integral A–Z markers in them. These are limited in their capacity, but very effective for current correspondence. Depending on the amount of your correspondence, you will have to clear your current file from time to time, still keeping it in alphabetical order and transferring it to storage files. These can be box-files, large manilla envelopes or even bundles tied with string. They should be marked with the dates covered.

You must have a clear-out now and then, but take care when scrapping correspondence. It is wise to retain anything relating to contracts, payments or controversial matters until they become definitely dead issues.

There are many commercial storage and filing systems. A good number of them are relatively expensive and often needlessly complex and fiddly. The methods I have described are both cheap and effective, even if you have tens of thousands of pictures and masses of research material. I have felt no need to change to anything more sophisticated.

Financial matters

Financial records must be accurate and understandable. You should have an account book in which you will note every expenditure associated with your writing and every payment received. I use the left-hand page for the expenditure and the right-hand page for the income.

I note the date of the expenditure, what the item was and to whom payment was made. The last column is for the amount. In an intermediate column, I record the amount paid for items which attract a Capital Allowance and I omit the amount in the end column. I shall cover this under Income Tax.

On the right-hand page I again note the date that payment was received, what it was for, who paid it and again the amount. I also reserve a column for any payments made to me for expenses. Although this will mainly apply to magazine articles, the publisher may well pay you for promotional expenses.

Your income may include fees for lectures or even TV appearances. You may also receive expenses as well as fees.

Keep all receipts associated with writing expenditures. Most suppliers will give you a detailed receipt, but all too often we seem to be handed barely legible print-outs from the till. I decipher these and staple them to a sheet of paper on which I write the details while they are fresh in my mind.

The receipts for the current financial year are kept together in yet another manilla envelope. Relevant receipts include those for phone, electricity, house insurance, heating and house maintenance. This aspect will also be covered under Income Tax.

Insurance

Although your writing equipment, such as typewriter, word-processor, photo-copier etc., come under normal household cover, anything taken out of the house requires special all-risks cover.

All-risks cover is necessary for cameras, portable typewriters, projectors for lecturing etc. Recently, I used my video-recorder to illustrate a lecture and suddenly realised that, if it were damaged, it would be uninsured for all-risks.

A word of warning about the insurance of photographic equipment. It is usually cheaper to obtain all-risks insurance under your household cover. However, some insurance companies insist that, if you sell photographs or use them to illustrate your writing, then you are a professional and require an appropriate separate policy. It could come as a very rude shock if, when you made a claim, you found that your expensive photographic equipment was, in fact, uninsured.

The simple answer is to write to your insurers and point out that you do sell photographs as incidental to your writing, or you hope to do so. If you are more deeply committed to taking photographs for sale, then say so. Ask for their assurance that your equipment is fully covered when being used for taking photographs for illustrating your work or for sale. Do not accept telephone reassurances, but insist on their reply in writing and then file it.

Other expenditures which writers might tend to forget are subscriptions to professional bodies, such as The Society of Authors, The Writers' Guild or The Royal Photographic Society. There is also the cost of research and reference books.

It is worth keeping a check on your phone calls made on writing business. You will probably be surprised at the high expenditure, particularly if you live in the provinces and phone London regularly. I timed my calls using my darkroom portable timer, until I had a fairly accurate idea of the proportion of business to private use.

Travelling and subsistence expenses on writing business should be recorded, together with the mileage of the car. See also under Income Tax.

Public Lending Rights

Under an Act of Parliament, writers receive a payment from public funds in proportion to the number of times their books were borrowed from public libraries in the year. Certain libraries are selected from which to take a representative sample of the incidence of borrowing. These libraries are regularly changed.

All writers should register their books for PLR. This can only be done after the date of publication, but it should be done as soon as possible. Application for registration should be made on the appropriate form, which can be obtained from: The Public Lending Right Office, Bayheath House, Prince Regent St, Stockton-on-Tees, Cleveland, TS18 1DF. An explanatory leaflet will be sent with the form.

The money allocated for PLR is divided between registered authors and this sum is subject to increase from time to time. Payments to popular authors can be fairly considerable, but there is an over-riding maximum, currently £6,000.

PLR is calculated on a year from July to June and payments are made in February of each year.

The entitlement to PLR is vested in the author, not the owner of the copyright. If, therefore, you were to sell the copyright, you should still register for PLR and enjoy its benefits.

The PLR system mainly uses the International Standard Book Numbers, ISBNs, to identify books. These numbers are normally printed on the biblio page of books and possibly on the covers also. It is important to note that different editions of a book, such as the hardback edition and the paperback edition, have different ISBNs and both must be registered for payment. Also, if your book is revised at a later date, the PLR office must be notified of the additional ISBN.

Self-sales

Income can also be derived from retailing your own books. Your contract will probably say that you can purchase books at the trade rate, but these are for your personal use only. If you wish to retail your book, you should write to the publisher and ask if you can do so. The publisher will usually agree, particularly if you have special outlets, such as lecture audiences. In some cases, the publisher may require you to register with them as a trade retailer.

Self-sales require extra records being kept. You must note all purchases and sales and, for tax purposes, you must take stock of books in hand for your annual accounts. The subject of self-sales is also covered in Chapter 13.

Income Tax

Everyone has a statutory liability to declare all sources of income to the Inland Revenue. As publishers notify the Inland Revenue of all payments to authors, any attempt to evade tax liability is not only illegal, it is also futile.

The Inland Revenue considers writers to be in one of two main categories, the professional writer or the casual writer. There is a third category, namely those who are employed as writers, but that is unlikely to concern most of us.

The borderline between the professional writer and the casual writer is ill-defined. As a rough guide, the professional writer would be expected to write fairly consistently even though he might have full-time employment in another capacity. Certainly, the Inland Revenue would expect the professional writer to make a profit.

Losses

In their early days, most writers find that they are writing at a loss. Their modest earnings, if any, are swallowed up by the expenses of research and they may have heavy capital outlay on typewriters or word-processors. Writers often reason that there is no need to bother with the Inland Revenue if they are not making a profit, but they would probably be wrong. In practice, declaring losses can pay off handsomely, particularly if your writing success is slow in coming.

You should write to the Inland Revenue office which normally handles your tax matters and tell them that you are trying to establish yourself as a writer. You should enclose a simple balance sheet showing your loss over the financial year and you should ask for this loss to be recorded.

Losses can be accumulated indefinitely, providing you are not asking for your losses to be used to offset your income from other taxable sources. Finally, when your writing does show a profit, all these accrued losses can be set against your writing earnings, often to your considerable benefit.

The need to keep an account book, together with all receipts, has been explained. It is unlikely that the Tax Inspector will ask to see your records at this stage, unless some evasion is suspected. However, it is essential that all records should be scrupulously maintained and presented in a logical and readable manner, in case they are called for.

Your balance sheet will probably resemble an abridged version of your account book. It will have expenditure on one side and receipts on the other. It is recommended that your receipts are itemised, but it is impractical to go into detail for your expenses. If, however, the Inland Revenue should require them, the details must be available.

For simplicity, it is usually preferable to claim a mileage rate for the use of your car on writing business. The appropriate rate, based on the running costs, can be ascertained by contacting the

Automobile Association and quoting the engine capacity of your car.

If you partly use a room in your house as a study for writing, some of the running costs of the house may be allowed as an expense. The expenses can include a proportion of the cost of some of the items already mentioned, namely heating, electricity, home insurance and maintenance. The proportion of these expenses which will be allowed is usually agreed with the Inspector.

It is important to claim for only part-use of the room. The exclusive use of a room could make you liable for possible Capital Gains Tax on ultimately selling the property. This is not a subterfuge, as it is unlikely that any room in a domestic house would not be used for a variety of purposes.

If you purchase new equipment to further your writing career, for example, camera, typewriter, photo-copier, word-processor, then you can claim a Capital Allowance.

Capital Allowance will usually be allowed in respect of purchases of equipment, as opposed to expendable items. Currently, in any financial year, the writer can claim an allowance of 25% of all purchases of appropriate equipment against the income from writing. In subsequent years, 25% of the balance may be claimed in each year until the balance is cleared. This is, in effect, a writing down process on the equipment purchased. If writers continue to show a loss, the balance could continue to grow until the accounts move into profit.

For example, if you bought a new word-processor for £600, a Capital Allowance of £150 could be set against your writing earnings. The balance of £450 would be carried forward and added to any Capital Allowance in the next financial year.

The system of Capital Allowances is a complex one and this description is, perhaps, an over-simplification. However, it should be sufficient to encourage writers to investigate thoroughly the entitlements associated with purchasing equipment for their work.

If your writing becomes a real success, then you may choose

to invest some of your profits to make life easier. This might include off-loading some of your financial problems to an accountant and your marketing worries and negotiations to an agent. If you can afford them, both of these professionals could increase your profitability and leave you more time for writing.

Before paying out for these services, you should be convinced that they are going to 'pay for their corn'. Is your current success going to be sustained or are you going to find yourself top-heavy with advisers, all taking a thick slice out of a small but precious cake?

If you decide to go ahead, try to find the best you can afford. Certainly, no writer can afford to select advisers from the bottom end of the scale. You can do no better than personal recommendation from a fellow-writer whose judgement you can trust.

Although this information on financial matters for writers is given in good faith, I am not an accountant and the ultimate responsibility for the writer's finances and tax returns must be his own.

Chapter Thirteen

On publication

Around publication day, you will receive your free copies of the book. There is a mistaken impression among non-writers that authors receive a vast quantity of free copies to be distributed liberally. This is not the case. The number of copies varies considerably from publisher to publisher and, possibly from author to author, but the numbers are always modest.

These copies are not for resale and most writers use them as gifts for the family, friends and those who made significant contributions to the publication of the book. You can always buy more copies at 'trade price'.

Promoting the book

The publisher will welcome your suggestions of those to whom complimentary copies of the book should be sent. These suggestions should be sent to the publisher well in advance of publication. They like to keep these to a minimum and you must not expect to use these copies to reward those who helped with the book. You will be expected to use your author's free copies for that purpose. The publisher's complimentary copies are primarily intended for reviewers and for those who are in a strong position to publicize the book, particularly such people as lecturers in the same subject as the book. Some of these copies have paid me handsome dividends, so think about them carefully.

Review copies go out to newspapers, magazines and other similar media which may be prepared to review the book, hopefully in glowing colours.

If the subject is specialised, there may be specialist magazines or even newsletters of specialist groups which might review the book. Their names and addresses should be passed to the publisher.

Nobody can be sure how wise an investment review copies are, but publishers seem convinced that it is worth it. All you lose are the royalties on all free books.

Depending on the initiative of your publisher's publicity department, you may be asked to make a personal contribution to a variety of promotional activities for your book. Certain types of book are more readily promoted than others. Some lend themselves to TV and radio broadcasts.

One of my books resulted in a TV chat show, two other TV appearances and several radio broadcasts, including being Richard Baker's guest on 'Start the Week'. There was also a personal appearance and book-signing at a public exhibition, together with other invitations to appear which I had to turn down due to pressure of work.

This type of publicity is demanding and, in most cases, results in rather modest fees, travelling expenses, perhaps an overnight stay in a hotel for an early morning programme. It is not very much for the stress and time involved, but it could increase sales considerably.

If you feel that this type of work is not for you, it is wise to tell your publisher from the beginning. For example, not everyone would wish to appear on TV. Although your contract will probably include your agreement to co-operate on publicity, this does not mean that you will be obliged to be available for any promotion the ingenuity of the publisher can arrange. In practice, the publisher will usually ask you if you will be available for a specific promotion and it is up to you to accept or decline, although you should not decline without good reason. Remember, this publicity is aimed at selling *your* book.

Publicity articles

One form of publicity, which can be useful and also profitable, is writing magazine articles on the subject of your book. Choose your magazine carefully and match your proposed article to it. It is important to find a magazine with a readership which is likely to be attracted to your book.

You should write a query letter to the editor proposing the article, stating your qualifications for writing it, if any. Of course, you must include the fact that your book on the subject is about to be published.

When submitting the article, ask for an editorial footnote, something along these lines: *The Complete Organic Gardener* by Charles Bloggs is published by New Nature Books at £5.95.

Remember that the article is intended as a promotion for your book. It should not only be an example of your best writing, but should also include some of the most appealing aspects of the book. If your book is illustrated, you can use any appropriate illustrations from the book in your article.

I believe this is a very powerful sales promotion because, if you have chosen your magazine carefully, you will be reaching the right market. The editor would not have bought the article unless he were sure that his readers would enjoy it. Those enjoying it are obviously potential readers of the book.

These articles should not be confined to around the time of publication. They can continue as long as the book is in print.

Press releases

When I have a new book published, I write a press release to promote it and send it to all local newspapers. A press release is a brief and succinct factual account of the author and his book. Your job is to present the facts in an interesting and attractive way. Firstly, it should appeal to the newspaper's editor as worth printing and, secondly, it should encourage the reader to go out and buy the book.

Few of us are likely to reach national newspapers with our press releases, but in the majority of areas there are a good number of local newspapers hungry for material.

You will already have given your publisher a list of the magazines and newspapers which you suggest should be given review copies. In your press release you should state that a review copy is being supplied, if that is the case. The editor may appreciate the press release when he comes to review the book.

The style of the press release must be plain and straightforward. It should be confined to one side of a single sheet, if possible. It should be double-spaced and given generous margins, like a conventional typescript, to facilitate editing.

I use the flexibility of my word-processor to print in bold and enlarged type the heading PRESS RELEASE. I then outline the salient facts about myself and the book. I always write it in the third person. I wind up with a note that photographs and further information are available and I give my name, address and phone number. I do not include a covering letter.

You should know all your local newspapers, including the free ones. If you are unsure, look at *Willing's Press Guide* in your library or even use Yellow Pages. The press release is useful publicity and only costs the price of the stamps.

I found out the name of the person who purchases the books for the libraries in my county. I write to her with the details of any new book on publication. I don't send a press release, but adopt a low key approach. I stress that I know that the library service is keen to promote the writing of local authors and that I know that there is a lot of local interest in the subject. If it is the case, I add that I shall be lecturing locally on the subject of the book and this is bound to generate interest among the libraries' readers.

This approach has worked well in the past and has never failed to stimulate the purchase of a good number of my books.

On publication you should apply for registration of your books for PLR, both hardback and paperback editions, if applicable. The details of this were given in Chapter 12, to which you should refer. Delay could lose you income.

Retail marketing

I have already referred to the income from self-sales. I explained the need to approach your publisher to ask for permission to retail your book. The income from such sales varies widely. It can range from selling a few copies to friends and acquaintances to selling hundreds of books at public lectures.

Expect to be given a discount of around 35% off the published price. Some publishers have more generous discounts for their authors, particularly if they buy large quantities.

One publisher allows authors to buy at half-price if ordering more than 100 copies. In addition to this profit, the author will get his royalties on each book.

You must not sell your books at less than the cover price. Under the Minimum Terms Agreement, it is illegal to do so. This is only waived if the book is remaindered or reduced in price by special agreement with the publisher, e.g. book club promotions.

The author wishing to sell his own books should always buy a modest number to start with. Books are expensive. They are also bulky and heavy. A lot of books can be a financial drain, particularly if they are selling slowly.

As most books are pre-packed, with the same number in each pack, it is a good idea to enquire how many books are in a pack and use the pack as your unit for ordering. One pack might cost several hundred pounds, so it would be wise not to order more than one initially. This is normally sent carriage paid.

Sales can be particularly easy if you lecture on your book's subject. Even small but enthusiastic groups can be surprisingly responsive. I recently lectured to a branch of The Women's Institute. It was very bad weather and only fifteen ladies turned up, but I still sold eight books.

If, as I do, you give a lecture accompanied by slides, it pays to have a slide of your book cover to show at the appropriate moment. You will, of course, offer to sign and dedicate books which are purchased.

As the author of a published book, you should use the fact to enhance your credibility to promote future acceptances and writing sales.

The fact that you have written a successful book can open other doors. For example, it could make you a more interesting proposition for an agent, should you want one. It will also make a publisher read your next book proposal a little more closely.

Reprints and revisions

After a while, it is to be hoped that your book will sell well enough to require reprinting. The first print-run of your first book is likely to be a cautious one and good sales will encourage an early reprint. This will be your opportunity to correct any overlooked typographical errors and make minor alterations. Sometimes fairly large and important revisions are necessary. These may be due to statutory or social changes, new technology, or previously unknown facts emerging. Such changes may require a revision rather than a reprint.

A revision means a major type-setting exercise, shifting passages and even adding pages. It is expensive and publishers like to avoid it if possible. Certainly, they would prefer to have the profits of several reprints before deciding that a revision is cost-effective. However, some of the factors I have mentioned could make the book inaccurate in its existing form and a revision might be unavoidable.

You should always keep a file noting any errors you come across or any points which would benefit from alteration or updating. The publisher will normally tell you if a reprint is planned, but it is wise to let him know that you will have some changes to suggest when a reprint becomes due.

Juggling effectively with a book's layout is a skilful business. You can point out the errors and leave it to the publisher to sort out or you can have a go at it yourself. I prefer the latter. I reason that the book is mine and I know what I am trying to express. Any revisions, I believe, should be in my words, not someone else's.

Remaindering

Remaindering a book is an unfortunate business for both publisher and author. It is sad to see a beautifully produced book, with full colour illustrations, being sold in the cut-price book shops for as little as a fifth of its cover price. It is even more tragic when it is your own book.

Your contract should make it clear that, not only should you be given advance notice that your book is to be remaindered, but you will be offered the option to buy the books at the best remaindered price. As the remaindered price is usually around 10% of the published price it could be a very good buy indeed, or it could be a white elephant.

If you have found by experience that you have steady self-sales for your book, it will clearly be wise to invest in some at the favourable price. Ask the publisher how many remain in stock. If the number is fairly large, be cautious about investing too much money. It will be capital which will not be earning interest. I know writers whose homes are cluttered up and groaning under the weight of unsold books. They curse the day that they invested in all those 10% bargains.

If you elect to buy a small quantity of the stock, the rest will go to the trade. You may find that you will be competing with bookshops at such a low price that your modest sales make the business not worth the effort.

Some writers with access to specialist markets have made a very good thing out of their remaindered books. They have advertised in the right places and sent out promotional pamphlets advertising the book at reduced prices and have had a worthwhile response. This should not be confused with an ordinary mail-shot. What is required is access to a list of, say, secretaries of clubs or associations whose members would be specially interested in the subject of your book. Offering the book at a discount to these secretaries could prove very profitable. However, I repeat, it is far better to underbuy than to overbuy and it pays to be cautious.

If your book is remaindered, it will no longer appear in Whitaker's *Books in print*. If you are retailing the book then it is important to get the book shown as still in print and obtainable from you. You should write to Whitaker's asking for a form of application. This should be completed and returned. There is no charge. (See list of useful addresses at the back of the book.)

Chapter Fourteen

Looking ahead

If you are serious about your writing, you will have given a great deal of thought to your next book long before the current one neared completion. I suggested that a good time to focus on the next one was when the finished typescript had been sent to the publisher. By the time your book is published, it is possible that you will have signed a new contract and will be well into writing the next one. That is how it should be done.

I am working on this, but I am planning three more ahead. These books have files which are growing all the time and even a broad synopsis of the first one is in hand. By the time this type-script is sent off, the chapter outline will be finished. As I mentioned earlier, this is to be a sponsored book and I already have sponsors lined up and willing to back it.

When considering your next book, there are questions you should ask yourself. Do I really want to write another book? Did I enjoy writing the last one or was it getting tedious? Have I drained the subject or is there enough material left for another book? Would I enjoy writing another on the same subject or do I really feel like starting something new?

Using the same subject, or aspects of it, has certain benefits. The research material is probably in hand and you are very familiar with it. You have proved your competence in that field, making it easier to get another contract.

You could use the material for writing a similar book, but for a different market. For example, if you wrote your first one for the expert, the next one might be for the man-in-the-street or for children.

Before starting a new book on the same subject, you should contact the publisher of the original one. Your contract is likely to state that you must not publish any abridgement or development of the first without offering it to the current publishers. In addition, you must not write anything which is likely to prejudice the sales of the first book. Exactly what might or might not prejudice these sales is debatable, but you must clear it with the publisher and get his consent in writing.

A sequel to the original book is another possibility. This book is a sort of sequel to my previous one, *The Way To Write Magazine Articles*. After all, writing non-fiction books is a logical progression from writing articles and the first one's success and early reprints made the idea of its sequel easy to sell to the publisher.

Whether you choose a variation of the same theme or a sequel, it is always sensible to consider sticking to your winning streak before embarking on an entirely new subject.

Have a chat with your publisher. Does he have anything in mind which could tie in either with your last book or with your style? If he suggests something, it will need no further sales pressure from you.

Always assuming that you are not a one-book author, for there are plenty of them about, that next one should be started promptly.

Too many writers sit back, well satisfied with their new success, and wait for the royalties to pour in. Unfortunately, unless you hit one of the rare jackpots, royalties will come in at a modest rate. The only way to improve matters is to have a good number of books published, all of which are generating royalties.

Each success brings new confidence, both in handling new subjects and in dealing with publishers. Ideas are often self-generating and you suddenly find that there are more opportunities than you can comfortably handle. It is now that you can, with all honesty, consider yourself a professional author.

Looking at new fields

You may decide that you would like to try other forms of non-fiction. The main specialised fields are writing for children, writing school text-books, writing for radio and writing for television.

Children's books

There is an excellent market for children's non-fiction. It is always worth considering whether your adult non-fiction book could be successfully rewritten for a younger age group. Of course, not every writer would want to write for children and even fewer would have the ability to do so.

It is often assumed that writing a children's book is easier than writing for adults. It is true that children's books are often shorter than the average adult non-fiction book, but they require no less skill and care than other books and many would say they require more.

To be a successful children's writer you need to have more than a little of the child in you. You must still be able to see the world as if through a child's eyes.

The need to hold the reader's attention throughout the book is essential, for children have a low threshold of boredom and are unwilling to plod through tedious passages.

A common mistake of authors new to the genre is to write down to children. This is disastrous and can only lead to rejection.

Many writers venture into children's books as a change from other writing and become totally hooked on it. From then on, they rarely if ever return to writing for adults.

School text-books

The best text-books command a huge market. Teachers are in a fine position to write these books. Not only are they well up in current educational trends and examination demands, but they will also have the practical teaching skills which should suggest the best methods of presenting the material in a palatable way.

Teachers with new ideas and clever presentation could find a very satisfying and lucrative opening. It is one which could continue after retirement, to provide a continuing interest and extra income. It could also be a welcome money-spinner for teachers who give up their careers, even temporarily to start a family, for example.

Writing for radio

To succeed in writing for radio, you must be an avid radio listener. It is the only way in which you can study the market, observe techniques and understand how the medium is used to put over material.

The markets are constantly changing and you must keep abreast of the needs. The best source of information is *Writing for the BBC* by BBC Publications. The book's blurb states: 'Never before has the BBC offered such a wide range of opportunities for the budding writer. It gives you details of the material required, how the script should be presented and to whom it should be sent.' As with most market publications, it is regularly revised. Make sure that you have an up-to-date copy.

It must be said that most of the opportunities are for writing drama rather than non-fiction, but a significant non-fiction market is there. The best opportunities are in features or documentaries. Ideas are usually submitted in brief outline, from which the writer may be invited to write a synopsis.

Writing for television

Much of what I have said about radio applies to TV. You must watch TV and particularly note programmes which are in the style that you feel you could handle. Sometimes, if your idea is adopted, you may be asked to take part in the programme yourself.

On one occasion, my idea was welcomed. I did the research, both written material and the legwork. Then my wife and I spent ten very hectic but fascinating days filming the documentary, about our work with bats. It really can happen, if you are prepared to go out of your way to make it do so.

The book referred to above, *Writing for the BBC*, covers TV as well as radio.

Improving your skills

Many writers are solitary creatures; after all, writing is a lonely business. Yet writing in isolation, without the stimulus from other writers, is not always the most productive for many of us. I enjoy meeting other writers from time to time, listening to their success stories, sharing their problems and comparing notes. It is a pleasure which many writers have discovered to be very valuable to their writing careers.

Throughout Britain there are Writers' Circles, the purpose of which is to discuss each other's work. The degree of help one can expect from a Writers' Circle varies with the skills of its membership. If you are interested, most Circles will welcome you for an evening to see if their activities suit your needs. A booklet with the current list of Writers' Circles is available from Jill Dick, Oldacre, Chapel-en-le-Frith, Derbyshire, SK12 6SY, current price £3, post free.

There are quite a number of regional summer schools and seminars available, where groups of writers have get-togethers, some more formal than others.

On a national scale, the long-established Writers' Summer School is probably the most famous of all international writers' conferences. Catering for 350 writers, it draws its members from all over the world. It is held in a comfortable conference centre in Derbyshire every August. It provides courses, lectures and discussion groups, as well as social activities. My wife and I have attended for the last sixteen years to date and consider it one of the highlights of our year. The fee at the time of writing is £120, full board, from Saturday to Friday.

In 1987, a similar activity was launched in Caerleon in the beautiful Usk Valley. Its title, Writers' Holiday, suggests its lower key approach, seeking a balance between holiday, lecture, discussion and coursework. It is held in July and the current fees are £105, full board, from Sunday to Friday.

Many writers attend both functions, particularly overseas visitors who find it very economical with the two courses only a week or so apart.

Writing courses are held in a wide range of adult further education colleges. Although fiction-writing tends to predominate, non-fiction is reasonably well covered. The quality of these courses varies and depends on the calibre of the tutor.

Details of adult further education college courses are available from NIACE, 19b, De Montfort St, Leicester, LE1 7GE, current price £1.50, including postage. One college at which my wife and I regularly tutor non-fiction writing courses and workshops is the excellent Maryland College, Woburn, Milton Keynes, MK17 9JD.

Most correspondence courses are expensive and, I believe, poor value for money. However, the Open College has a course for beginners entitled The Writers' Course and priced at a modest £25.

One of the best ways of progressing is to read and write. Read the work of top writers whose fields are similar to your own interests. When a book impresses you, try to analyse it and discover the secret of its appeal. How is the book structured and its chapters developed? Does the author use dialogue and, if so, how does he handle it?

Writing is like any other skill – improvement requires practice. You should try to write something every day, even if it fails to satisfy your critical eye. Most writers find that writing something, no matter how inadequate it may seem, helps to lubricate the writer's flow of words. Writing doggedly, even when you don't feel like it, is probably one of the best ways of overcoming writer's block.

It would be true to say that no writer ever masters his craft. He improves, of course, but perfection in writing is unattainable. Most of us will never reach great heights; it must suffice to do our best and constantly try to improve.

Those of you who have written your first book will have a great deal to learn, but you can rest assured that you are well on the way. Keep writing; stick to your principles; be professional, and continuing success will be well within your capabilities.

Useful addresses

British Printing Industry Federation,
11 Bedford Row,
London WC1R 4DX.

National Institute of Adult Continuing Education,
19B De Montfort St,
Leicester LE1 7GE.

Public Lending Rights,
Bayheath House,
Prince Regent St,
Stockton-on-Tees,
Cleveland TS18 1DF.

Society of Authors,
84 Drayton Gdns,
London SW10 9SB.

Society of Indexers,
16 Green Rd,
Birchington,
Kent CT7 9JZ.

Whitaker's Booklisting Services,
12 Dyott St,
London WC1A 1DF.

Writers' Guild of Great Britain,
430 Edgware Rd,
London W2 1EH.

Writers' Holiday,
Mrs Ann Hobbs,
30 Pant Rd,
Newport,
Gwent NP9 5PR.

Writers' Summer School,
Mrs Philippa Boland,
The Red House,
Mardens Hill,
Crowborough,
Sussex TN6 1XN.